Understanding Time

An Exploration

A Beginner's Guide to the
Concepts and Theories of Time

Peter Kattan

Petra Books
www.petrabooks.com

ISBN - 979-8-8691-8385-9

Preface

Welcome to Understanding Time - An Exploration: A Beginner's Guide to the Concepts and Theories of Time. In this captivating journey through the intricate tapestry of time, we embark on a quest to unravel one of the most enigmatic mysteries of the universe. Time, an omnipresent force shaping our reality, has fascinated thinkers, scientists, and philosophers for millennia. Yet, despite our ceaseless efforts, it remains an elusive concept, transcending our grasp. This book endeavors to demystify time, offering a comprehensive overview accessible to all curious minds, regardless of their background in science or philosophy.

Time, in its essence, is a fundamental aspect of existence. It permeates every facet of our lives, dictating the rhythm of our days, the flow of events, and the progression of ages. But what is time? Is it a mere illusion, a construct of the human mind? Or does it possess an objective reality independent of our perception? These questions lie at the heart of our exploration.

We begin our journey by delving into the nature of time itself. Drawing upon insights from physics, philosophy, and psychology, we navigate through the various conceptualizations of time throughout history. From the ancient Greeks' notion of Kairos to Einstein's revolutionary theory of relativity, we trace the evolution of our understanding, shedding light on the diverse perspectives that have shaped our perception of time.

As we venture deeper into the mysteries of temporality, we confront paradoxes and puzzles that challenge our intuitive understanding. The arrow of time, the passage from past to future, seems to defy the immutable laws of physics. From the enigma of causality to the elusive concept of time dilation, we confront phenomena that stretch the boundaries of our imagination.

But time is not merely a scientific abstraction; it is also intimately intertwined with our human experience. We explore the psychological dimension of time, uncovering the ways in which our perception of time shapes our memories, emotions, and sense of self. From the fleeting moments of joy to the relentless march of aging, we confront the profound implications of temporality on the human condition.

In the final stretch of our journey, we chart the horizons of time, probing the frontiers of theoretical physics and speculative philosophy. From the tantalizing prospect of time travel to the mind-bending concepts of multiverse theory, we confront speculative ideas that push the boundaries of our understanding.

But amidst the uncertainty and speculation, one thing remains clear: the quest to understand time is a journey without end. As we conclude our exploration, we are reminded that our understanding of time is constantly evolving, shaped by new discoveries, insights, and perspectives. Whether you are a novice seeking an introduction to the concepts of time or a seasoned scholar in search of new insights, this book invites you to embark on a journey of discovery, to unravel the mysteries of time and glimpse the profound beauty of existence.

Note that a major part of the text in this book was written with the help of artificial intelligence.

Peter Kattan   March 2024

Contents

Understanding Time - An Exploration
A Beginner's Guide to the Concepts and Theories of Time

Chapter One:
Nature of Time

The nature of time is a subject of philosophical and scientific inquiry that has been debated for centuries. Time can be defined as a concept that allows us to order events and experiences, measure the duration of events, and understand the progression of events.

From a scientific perspective, time is typically considered to be a dimension in which events occur in a linear progression. It is also considered to be relative, meaning that its rate of progression can vary depending on the relative velocity of the observer. According to Einstein's theory of relativity, time slows down in the presence of a strong gravitational field and speeds up when an object is moving at high speeds.

From a philosophical perspective, time is often seen as an illusion. Some philosophers argue that time is an abstraction created by the human mind and has no objective existence in the world. They argue that events do not occur in time but rather that time is a framework in which events are organized and understood.

Despite ongoing debates about the nature of time, most scientists and philosophers agree that time is a fundamental aspect of our existence. It shapes our experiences, influences our actions, and provides a structure for understanding the world around us. Ultimately, the nature of time remains a mystery, but it continues to be a subject of intense inquiry and speculation.

Time is a concept that is fundamental to our understanding of the world, but its nature is still a topic of much debate and discussion among philosophers, physicists, and scientists.

Some people view time as an absolute and unchanging entity, while others see it as a human construct that is relative to the observer.

From a physical perspective, time is often defined as the measurement of the duration between two events. It is a continuous, irreversible flow that allows us to order events and understand causality. Physicists have discovered that time is not absolute and can be influenced by various factors, such as gravity and velocity. This led to the development of the theory of general relativity, which shows that time can be distorted and even appear to slow down or speed up in certain conditions.

In contrast, many philosophers argue that time is a human-made concept that we use to structure our experiences and understand causality. They argue that time does not exist in a objective sense, but is instead a way for us to make sense of the world and our experiences within it. This view suggests that time is not a fundamental aspect of the universe, but is instead a way of ordering events and giving meaning to our experiences.

One of the main debates surrounding the nature of time is whether it is a physical entity or a mental construct. Some physicists believe that time is a physical dimension, just like space, while others argue that it is a human invention that is used to describe the progression of events. Similarly, philosophers have long debated whether time is a real aspect of the world or simply a product of our subjective experiences.

Despite these debates, there is no doubt that time plays a central role in our lives and in the functioning of the universe. It is an essential aspect of our experience of the world and provides a framework for understanding causality and change. Whether time is a fundamental aspect of the universe or simply a human invention, it remains one of the most fascinating and mysterious aspects of our world.

Chapter Two:
Definition of Time

Time is a concept that has been a subject of fascination and study for thousands of years. Despite its seemingly simple definition, time is a complex and multifaceted idea that is difficult to fully understand and explain.

At its most basic level, time can be defined as the measurement of the duration between two events. This definition is often used in physics and science, where time is seen as a continuous and irreversible flow that allows us to order events and understand causality. In this sense, time is seen as a physical dimension that is separate from space, and is used to describe the progression of events in the universe.

However, time is not just a physical entity, but also a human construct that is used to give meaning to our experiences. In this sense, time can be thought of as a mental or psychological concept that allows us to organize our experiences and understand our place in the world. Time is often used to describe the sequence of events and the progression of history, and is a central aspect of our experiences of the world.

In philosophy, time is a topic of much debate and discussion. Some philosophers argue that time is a real aspect of the world, while others believe that it is simply a human invention used to make sense of our experiences. There are also philosophical debates about the nature of time, including questions about whether time is absolute or relative, and whether it flows in one direction or is cyclical.

Time is a complex and multifaceted concept that has been the subject of much debate and study for thousands of years.

Whether it is seen as a physical dimension, a human construct, or a combination of both, time is an essential aspect of our experiences of the world and plays a central role in the functioning of the universe. Despite its many definitions and interpretations, time remains one of the most fascinating and mysterious aspects of our world.

Time is a concept used to sequence events, to compare the duration of events, and to quantify the motions of objects. It is often considered a continuous sequence of events that progress from the past through the present to the future. Physically, time can be defined as a dimension in which events occur in a linear sequence. The measurement of time is essential in many fields, including physics, astronomy, engineering, and commerce. The most widely accepted definition of time in physics is as a dimension in which events occur in a linear sequence. However, the true nature of time remains one of the greatest mysteries in science and philosophy.

In physics, time is often considered to be a fundamental aspect of the universe and is defined as a scalar quantity (a single value, as opposed to a vector quantity which has both magnitude and direction). It is an independent dimension, meaning it is not relative to other dimensions or properties of the universe. The concept of time is also related to the concept of causality, which states that an event (the cause) must occur before another event (the effect) can occur.

Time is a relative concept and its measurement is dependent on the observer's frame of reference. In Einstein's theory of relativity, time can appear to slow down or speed up, relative to a different observer. This is known as time dilation.

In philosophy, time has been the subject of much debate and discussion, with different philosophical schools of thought offering different definitions and interpretations of the concept. Some philosophers argue that time is a real, objective property of the universe, while others argue that it is a subjective experience created by human perception.

Regardless of the exact definition or interpretation, the concept of time is fundamental to our understanding of the world and plays a critical role in many aspects of our daily lives.

Time is a concept that is essential to our understanding of the world and our experiences within it. It is often defined as a dimension in which events occur in a linear progression and can be measured by the duration between events.

In physics, time is considered to be a fundamental aspect of the universe, and it is closely related to space and motion. It is a dimension in which events occur in a sequence and can be measured by clocks and other devices. Time is also considered to be relative, meaning that its rate of progression can vary depending on the observer's relative velocity and proximity to a gravitational field.

Regardless of how one defines it, time plays a crucial role in our lives. It provides a framework for ordering and understanding events, it allows us to measure the duration of experiences, and it influences our perception of the world around us. Time is a fundamental aspect of existence and a subject that continues to be explored and debated by scientists, philosophers, and people from all walks of life.

Chapter Three:
Importance of Understanding the Nature of Time

Time is a fundamental concept that has been central to human understanding for thousands of years. From the earliest moments of human history, people have sought to understand time and measure its passage. In modern times, the concept of time has become even more important as we rely on it to keep track of everything from appointments and meetings to international travel schedules and financial transactions. Understanding the nature of time is essential in order to use it effectively and make the most of its many benefits.

One of the most important aspects of time is its role in measuring change and progress. Time provides a means of measuring how long it takes for things to happen, and this information is critical for understanding the world around us. For example, time helps us to understand the speed of chemical reactions, the movement of celestial bodies, and the evolution of living organisms. Understanding time is also important in our personal lives, as it enables us to plan and coordinate activities and to keep track of important events and milestones.

Another important aspect of time is its role in creating order and structure. Time provides a framework for organizing and prioritizing our activities and helps us to manage our resources more effectively. For example, knowing the time of day, we can determine when it is best to rest or work, when to eat and sleep, and when to pursue leisure activities. Time also provides a means of measuring the duration of events, and this information is essential for determining the pace and rhythm of our lives.

A further benefit of understanding the nature of time is that it helps us to understand cause and effect. Time allows us to understand the sequence of events that led to a particular outcome, and this information is crucial for problem- solving and decision-making. By analyzing the timing of events, we can often identify patterns and correlations that would not be apparent.

Understanding the nature of time is essential for making the most of its many benefits. Time provides a means of measuring change and progress, creating order and structure, and understanding cause and effect. By gaining a deeper understanding of time, we can use it more effectively to manage our lives and the world around us.

One of the key philosophical debates surrounding time is the relationship between time and reality. Some philosophers argue that time is a real and independent entity, while others argue that it is merely a human construct. This debate is important because it affects how we understand the nature of the universe and our place within it.

Another important philosophical aspect of time is the relationship between past, present, and future. Time is often described as a continuous flow, with events unfolding one after the other in an irreversible sequence. However, some philosophers have argued that time is not continuous, and that events exist in the present moment only. This debate is important because it affects our understanding of causality, free will, and the meaning of human existence.

Understanding the nature of time can also have spiritual and religious implications. Many spiritual and religious traditions view time as a fundamental aspect of the universe, and hold beliefs about the cyclical nature of time, the existence of a cosmic timeline, and the idea of reincarnation.

Understanding the nature of time can help us to understand our place in the cosmos and the meaning of our existence.

The nature of time is essential for understanding the world around us, as well as for exploring the philosophical and existential implications of this concept. By continuing to explore the mysteries of time, we can gain a deeper understanding of our place in the universe and the meaning of human existence.

From a scientific perspective, time is typically viewed as a dimension in which events occur in a linear progression. Physicists have developed theories that describe how time behaves in different contexts, including Einstein's theory of relativity, which describes how time behaves in the presence of strong gravitational fields and at high speeds. These theories have helped us to better understand the nature of time, but they have also raised new questions and challenges.

From a philosophical perspective, time has been seen as both an objective, independent aspect of the universe and a subjective human invention. Some philosophers argue that time is a fundamental aspect of reality, while others see it as an illusion created by the human mind. This debate continues to be a topic of ongoing inquiry, and new theories and perspectives continue to emerge.

Despite the ongoing debates and questions surrounding the nature of time, it is clear that time plays a crucial role in our lives. It provides a framework for ordering and understanding events, it allows us to measure the duration of experiences, and it influences our perception of the world around us. To truly understand the nature of time, it is necessary to consider both scientific and philosophical perspectives, and to continue exploring and questioning the nature of this fundamental aspect of existence.

Chapter Four:
Ancient Views on Time

Ancient civilizations had diverse views on time and its measurement. Some civilizations, such as the Mayans and the Egyptians, had complex calendars based on astronomical observations.

The Mayans, who lived in Central America, developed a highly accurate calendar that was divided into units of days, months, and years. The Mayans believed that time was cyclical and that the universe went through cycles of creation and destruction. This idea was reflected in their calendar, which was based on a series of interlocking cycles.

The Egyptians, who lived along the Nile River in Africa, also had a complex calendar based on astronomical observations. They divided the year into 12 months of 30 days each, with an additional five days added at the end of the year. The Egyptians believed that time was linear, moving forward from the creation of the world to the end of the world. They saw the sun as a symbol of the passage of time and associated it with the god Ra.

In ancient China, time was seen as a crucial aspect of life and was closely tied to the concept of fate. The Chinese believed that time was linear and that each person had a predetermined destiny that was determined by the time and place of their birth. They developed a lunar calendar that was based on the cycles of the moon and was used for both religious and agricultural purposes.

The ancient Greeks had a more philosophical view of time. They believed that time was an abstract concept that was connected to the natural cycles of the universe. They saw time as a constant, unchanging aspect of the world that was independent of human actions. The Greek philosopher Aristotle, for example, argued that time was a measure of change, and that the passage of time was indicated by the movement of the sun, moon, and stars.

Ancient civilizations had diverse views on time, its measurement, and its significance. Some civilizations saw time as cyclical, while others saw it as linear. Some civilizations saw time as closely tied to the concept of fate, while others saw it as an abstract concept independent of human actions. Regardless of their views, however, all of these civilizations recognized the importance of time and made efforts to measure and understand it.

In ancient India, time was seen as a fundamental aspect of reality and was closely tied to the concept of karma. The ancient Indian scriptures, such as the Vedas and the Purina's, described time as being cyclical in nature, with an endless cycle of creation and destruction. The ancient Indians developed a complex system of time measurement, including the concept of the yuga, which was a cycle of time that lasted thousands of years. They also believed in the idea of reincarnation, in which the soul was reborn after death, which further emphasized the cyclical nature of time.

In Mesopotamia, which was located in the region that is now modern-day Iraq, time was seen as a tool for measuring the passage of events. The ancient Mesopotamians developed a lunar calendar that was used for religious and agricultural purposes. They believed that the movements of the moon were closely tied to the passage of time, and they used the phases of the moon to mark the passage of time.

The ancient Persians, who lived in what is now Iran, had a cyclical view of time and believed in the concept of eternity.

They saw time as being cyclical and believed that history repeated itself in endless cycles. The Persian philosopher Zoroaster, for example, believed that the world would eventually come to an end and then be recreated again. This idea was reflected in their calendar, which was based on the cycles of the moon and the sun.

In ancient Rome, time was seen as a tool for measuring the passage of events and for regulating daily life. The Romans developed a solar calendar that was based on the cycles of the sun, and they used it to regulate the timing of religious and civil events. They also believed in the idea of the "eternal present," in which the present moment was seen as a point of balance between the past and the future.

Ancient civilizations had diverse views on time and its significance. Some civilizations saw time as cyclical, while others saw it as linear. Some civilizations saw time as closely tied to the concept of fate, while others saw it as a tool for measuring the passage of events. Regardless of their views, however, all of these civilizations recognized the importance of time and made efforts to measure and understand it.

In ancient Babylonia, time was seen as a fundamental aspect of the universe and was closely tied to astronomical observations. The ancient Babylonians developed a lunar calendar that was based on the cycles of the moon, and they used it to regulate the timing of religious and agricultural events. They believed that the movements of the moon were closely tied to the passage of time and used the phases of the moon to mark the passage of time.

In ancient Mesoamerica, time was seen as cyclical and was closely tied to astronomical observations. The Mayans, Aztecs, and other Mesoamerican civilizations developed complex calendars that were based on astronomical observations and that marked the cycles of time. These calendars were used for religious and agricultural purposes, and they helped these civilizations to understand and regulate the timing of the natural world.

In ancient Japan, time was seen as a fundamental aspect of the universe and was closely tied to the concept of fate. The ancient Japanese believed in the idea of reincarnation and saw time as cyclical in nature, with an endless cycle of birth, death, and rebirth. They developed a lunar calendar that was used for religious and agricultural purposes, and they used it to regulate the timing of the natural world.

Chapter Five:
Evolution of Time in Western Philosophy

The evolution of the concept of time in Western philosophy is a long and complex history, which spans from ancient Greece to modern-day theories. In the early Greek philosophy, time was seen as an objective reality, independent of human experience and consciousness. This view was held by philosophers like Parmenides and Zeno, who believed that time was an unchanging and eternal entity that flowed uniformly.

However, with the advent of the atomistic philosophy, the concept of time underwent a major transformation. Philosophers like Democritus and Epicurus held the view that time was a product of the motion of atoms and was therefore dependent on physical processes. This view marked a shift from the idea of time as an absolute and independent entity to a more relative and subjective concept.

The medieval philosophy of the Christian Church saw time as a creation of God, with a beginning and an end. Saint Augustine, one of the most influential thinkers of this period, saw time as a continuous flow of moments, each of which was dependent on God's will. This view was in line with the dominant belief that God was the creator and sustainer of the universe, and that time was part of his creation.

The Scientific Revolution of the 16th and 17th centuries saw the rise of a more mechanistic view of time. Philosophers like René Descartes and Isaac Newton saw time as a linear, absolute and continuous entity, which could be measured and quantified using mathematical methods. This view of time dominated the scientific community for centuries and remains the dominant view among physicists to this day.

However, with the advent of Einstein's theory of relativity, the concept of time underwent yet another transformation. Einstein showed that time was not a linear and absolute entity, but was relative to the observer's state of motion. This challenged the long-held view of time as a fixed and universal entity, and led to a more nuanced understanding of the nature of time.

In recent times, the concept of time has been subjected to further scrutiny in the fields of philosophy and physics. Philosophers like Martin Heidegger and Jean-Paul Sartre have explored the relationship between time and human existence, while physicists like Julian Barbour and Lee Smolin have questioned the very foundations of the classical view of time.

The evolution of the concept of time in Western philosophy reflects the changing perspectives and understandings of the nature of the universe and human experience. From ancient Greece to modern physics, the concept of time has undergone numerous transformations, each of which has contributed to a more nuanced and sophisticated understanding of this elusive and fundamental aspect of our reality.

The developments outlined in the previous response, the concept of time has also been a central topic in existentialist philosophy. For example, Martin Heidegger saw time as a fundamental aspect of human existence, arguing that it was not just a property of the physical world, but was also a part of human being's own essence. He saw time as an ontological category that was irreducible to physics and could not be understood solely in terms of physical processes.

In the 20th century, the concept of time was also the subject of intense debate in the philosophy of physics. In particular, the advent of quantum mechanics and the theory of general relativity led to the realization that the classical view of time as a linear and continuous entity was no longer tenable. This led to the development of new theories and perspectives, such as the concept of time as a quantum mechanical operator and the idea of time as an emergent property of the physical world.

In recent years, the concept of time has also been the subject of interdisciplinary research, bringing together insights from philosophy, physics, psychology, and neuroscience. For example, the philosophy of time has been linked to the study of consciousness, with some theorists suggesting that the experience of time may be a fundamental aspect of subjective experience. The study of time has also been linked to the development of new technologies, such as quantum computing and the potential for time travel.

Overall, the evolution of the concept of time in Western philosophy reflects the changing perspectives and understandings of the nature of reality. From the ancient Greeks to contemporary interdisciplinary research, the concept of time has been subject to ongoing exploration and reinterpretation, reflecting the quest for a deeper understanding of the world and our existence.

The idea of time has also played a significant role in the development of metaphysics, which is concerned with the fundamental nature of reality. In particular, the concept of time has been closely tied to debates about the nature of causation and the existence of an objective reality independent of human experience.

For example, some philosophers have argued that time is necessary for the existence of causation, as cause and effect must occur in a temporal sequence. Others have challenged this view, suggesting that time may be a product of human experience, rather than an objective reality. This has led to debates about the nature of time itself, with some philosophers suggesting that time may be an illusion or that it exists in a non-linear and non-standard manner.

Another important aspect of the concept of time in Western philosophy is its relationship to space. From the ancient Greeks to modern-day physics, the nature of time and space has been closely intertwined, with philosophers and scientists seeking to understand the interplay between these two fundamental aspects of reality. For example, Einstein's theory of special relativity showed that space and time were not independent entities, but were interrelated and could be described by a single four-dimensional space-time.

In recent years, the concept of time has also been the subject of debate in the philosophy of science, with some theorists challenging the traditional view of science as a linear and cumulative process. For example, some have argued that science is not a simple accumulation of knowledge, but is shaped by historical, social, and cultural factors. This has led to a reevaluation of the role of time in scientific inquiry and the development of new approaches to the study of science and its history.

The concept of time has been a central topic in Western philosophy for centuries and has been the subject of ongoing exploration and debate. The evolution of the concept of time reflects changing perspectives on the nature of reality, the intricate interplay between time and causation, underscores.

Chapter Six :
Evolution of Time Concept

The concept of time has been a subject of philosophical inquiry for centuries, with a diverse range of opinions and perspectives emerging over time. In Western philosophy, the evolution of the concept of time can be traced back to ancient Greece and has continued to evolve through the medieval period, the Enlightenment, and into modern times.

In ancient Greece, the philosopher Aristotle believed that time was a measure of change, and that time itself did not change. This view was later challenged by the philosopher Zeno of Elea, who argued that time was an illusion and that the universe was eternal and unchanging.

During the medieval period, the philosopher St. Augustine of Hippo developed a concept of time that saw it as quality of God, and not something that exists in the physical world. Augustine saw time as a series of present moments, each of which is created by God.

The Enlightenment brought a new perspective on time, with the philosopher Immanuel Kant viewing time as a necessary condition for the existence of the physical world. Kant argued that time was a priori, meaning that it was known independently of experience, and that it was a necessary part of our understanding of the world.

In modern times, the concept of time has been further explored by philosophers such as Henri Bergson, who saw time as a creative force that was essential to the evolution of life and the universe. Bergson argued that time was not just a measure of change, but was itself a form of change, and that it was constantly flowing and evolving.

The evolution of the concept of time in Western philosophy has been marked by a range of differing perspectives, from the view of time as a measure of change in ancient Greece, to the view of time as a quality of God in the medieval period, to the view of time as a necessary condition for the existence of the physical world in the Enlightenment, to the view of time as a creative force in modern times. Despite these differing perspectives, the concept of time continues to be a central and enduring subject of philosophical inquiry.

The concept of time has also been explored in the realm of physics, particularly with the advent of Einstein's theory of relativity. According to Einstein, time is not absolute and unchanging, but is relative to the observer and can be affected by the observer's velocity and gravity. This challenged the traditional Newtonian view of time as a universal and absolute entity.

Another important development in the concept of time was the introduction of the idea of the "arrow of time." This concept refers to the idea that time has a direction and that events occur in a definite sequence, from past to present to future. The arrow of time is a fundamental aspect of our experience of the world and has been the subject of much philosophical and scientific inquiry.

In recent years, the concept of time has also been explored in the context of quantum mechanics. In this framework, time is seen as a dynamic and interconnected aspect of the universe, and its relationship to space, matter, and energy is still being explored.

Also to its scientific and philosophical implications, the concept of time has also had a significant impact on our culture and our understanding of the world. For example, the idea of linear time has shaped our sense of progress and history, while the concept of cyclical time has been central to many religious and spiritual traditions.

The evolution of the concept of time in Western philosophy has been marked by a rich and diverse range of perspectives, from the ancient Greeks to modern physics and beyond. Despite its many contradictions and complexities, the concept of time continues to be a central and enduring subject of inquiry for philosophers, scientists, and people from all walks of life.

The study of time has also been incorporated into various fields such as psychology, where time perception, the subjective experience of time, has been studied. It has been found that time perception can vary depending on a person's mood, attention, and level of arousal, and that time perception can be influenced by many factors such as age, culture, and personal experiences.

Another area where the concept of time has been studied is the philosophy of history, which deals with the meaning, purpose, and nature of historical events and their relationship to time. This field of inquiry raises questions about the role of time in shaping human events, the nature of historical causality, and the possibility of predicting the future based on past events.

The concept of time also has implications for ethics and moral philosophy, as it relates to the nature of free will, responsibility, and justice. For example, if time is seen as flowing in a linear and irreversible manner, then it becomes difficult to imagine a world in which people can have genuine free will and are fully responsible for their actions.

Ultimately, the exploration of time finds resonance within the realms of spirituality and religion, where diverse traditions offer unique interpretations and insights into its essence and its relationship to the divine and the afterlife. For example, some religious traditions view time as cyclical and see the world as constantly repeating itself, while others view time as linear and see it as leading to an ultimate endpoint.

The concept of time has far-reaching implications for a wide range of disciplines and areas of inquiry. Whether viewed as a measure of change, a necessary condition for the physical world, a creative force, or something that is relative and subjective, time remains a central and mysterious aspect of our existence that continues to inspire philosophical and scientific inquiry.

Chapter Seven:
Science Shaping Time Understanding

Science has played a significant role in shaping our understanding of time. The concept of time has been an enigma for humans for thousands of years, with early civilizations attempting to measure and understand it. However, it was not until the development of science that we began to truly comprehend its nature.

Isaac Newton made a seminal contribution to our comprehension of time through his groundbreaking work, "Philosophiæ Naturalis Principia Mathematica." Within its pages, Newton not only elucidated the fundamental laws of motion and gravitation but also conceptualized time as an unbroken, absolute entity, devoid of influence from external occurrences. This notion, defining time as a seamless and unchanging continuum, became the cornerstone of classical mechanics, reigning supreme in scientific circles for more than two centuries.

However, the advent of Einstein's theory of special and general relativity challenged Newton's view of time. Einstein's theories showed that time is not an absolute quantity, but is relative to the observer. This meant that the speed of time could be affected by gravity and motion, leading to the famous concept of "time dilation."

Additionally, quantum mechanics, the branch of physics that deals with the behavior of matter and energy at a subatomic level, has also had an impact on our understanding of time. The principles of quantum mechanics state that time cannot be accurately measured at a subatomic level, as time and space are inextricably linked.

Science has greatly advanced our understanding of time. From classical mechanics to relativity and quantum mechanics, science has shown us that time is not a simple, uniform concept but a complex, relative one. This increased understanding has allowed us to make new discoveries and advancements in fields such as astronomy and computer science, and will continue to shape our understanding of the world in the future.

In recent years, the study of time has become a multidisciplinary field, with contributions from physics, philosophy, psychology, and other sciences. For example, psychological studies have shown that our perception of time is not consistent, and can vary depending on our mental and emotional state. This has led to a new understanding of how our brains process time and how this affects our daily lives.

In physics, the study of time has also led to new discoveries in the field of cosmology. The concept of time is central to our understanding of the universe and its evolution. For instance, scientists have used observations of the cosmic microwave background radiation and the large-scale structure of the universe to estimate the age of the universe, which is now estimated to be around 13.8 billion years old.

The study of time has also had practical applications in many fields. For instance, in engineering and computer science, the accurate measurement of time is essential for the functioning of GPS systems, communication networks, and many other technologies.

Moreover, science has helped to dispel myths and superstitions about time that were prevalent in many cultures for centuries. For instance, the idea that time is cyclical, as opposed to linear, was prevalent in many ancient cultures, but has been disproven by modern science.

The role of science in shaping our understanding of time has been immense. Science has provided us with a deeper, more nuanced understanding of this concept and has had far-reaching implications for many areas of our lives. As scientific knowledge continues to advance, our understanding of time will continue to evolve and deepen, leading to new discoveries and advancements.

Furthermore, the study of time has also had a profound impact on our understanding of the nature of reality. For example, the concept of time as a dimension, similar to space, has challenged our traditional view of the world as a collection of objects in a static and unchanging environment. Instead, science has shown us that time and space are intertwined, forming the fabric of the universe and shaping the way it evolves.

Moreover, the study of time has also shed light on the nature of causality, or the relationship between cause and effect. This has led to a deeper understanding of the causal structure of the universe, and how events are connected through cause and effect.

Science has also advanced our understanding of the relationship between time and consciousness. For example, studies have shown that our subjective experience of time is shaped by our perception, attention, and memory. This has led to new theories about the nature of consciousness and the way it relates to time.

The study of time has also had implications for our understanding of the meaning of life. For instance, the fact that time is irreversible and that the future is not predetermined has led to new philosophical debates about free will, determinism, and the meaning of existence.

The study of time has been a central area of inquiry for science, with far-reaching implications for our understanding of the world and our place in it. Science has revealed that time is a complex and multi-faceted concept, shaping our perception of reality and influencing many aspects of our lives. The study of time will continue to be an important area of investigation, leading to new discoveries and advancements in the future.

Chapter Eight:
Understanding of Time Has Evolved Over Time

Time is a fundamental aspect of our lives. It governs the events that occur in our daily routines, shapes the way we think about the past, present, and future, and influences our perceptions of the world around us. However, our understanding of time has evolved significantly over the centuries, shaped by the advances of science and technology, as well as the cultural and philosophical beliefs of different civilizations.

In ancient civilizations, time was often seen as cyclical, with events recurring in an endless cycle. This view was prevalent in cultures such as the Babylonians, who believed that time was controlled by the movements of the planets, and the ancient Greeks, who viewed time as a divine force that was beyond human control.

Religious and philosophical beliefs also played a significant role in shaping views of time. In many cultures, time was seen as a linear progression, with a beginning and an end, and a divine force that guided the universe towards its ultimate destiny.

The Scientific Revolution of the 16th and 17th centuries marked a turning point in our understanding of time. The work of scientists such as Galileo Galilei and Isaac Newton helped to establish a more empirical and rational understanding of time and its relationship to the physical universe.

The development of the clock during this period had a profound impact on our understanding of time, providing a way to measure and standardize time that was independent of the natural cycles of the sun and the stars. This paved the way for the development of modern timekeeping and the widespread use of clocks and calendars.

The theory of relativity, proposed by Albert Einstein in the early 20th century, revolutionized our understanding of time and space. Einstein's theory showed that time and space were not separate entities, but rather interrelated aspects of a single four-dimensional space-time. This provided a framework for understanding the behavior of time and space in different physical contexts, and for explaining the effects of gravity and the curvature of space- time.

The concept of time in quantum mechanics has also had a significant impact on our understanding of time. In quantum mechanics, time is treated as a continuous parameter, similar to the dimensions of space. However, the theory also suggests that the behavior of particles on a quantum level is not predictable, which challenges our traditional notions of causality and time.

The relationship between time and consciousness has been a topic of ongoing debate and investigation. Some researchers have explored the possibility that the subjective experience of time is tied to physical processes in the brain, and that the perception of time is influenced by a range of factors, including attention, memory, and sensory input.

Our understanding of time has evolved significantly over the centuries, shaped by the advances of science and technology, as well as the cultural and philosophical beliefs of different civilizations. From the cyclical views of time in ancient civilizations, to the physical approach to time in modern science, our understanding of time has undergone a transformation that has helped us to better understand the world around us and our place in it.

It's worth noting that the evolution of our understanding of time has not only had implications for our understanding of the physical world, but also for our philosophical and cultural perspectives. The idea that time is a fundamental aspect of our lives has given rise to numerous questions about the nature of existence and the meaning of life, and has been a source of inspiration for artists, writers, and musicians throughout history.

One of the most enduring philosophical questions about time is whether time is absolute or relative. The idea that time is relative suggests that time is a human construct, and that it only exists in the mind, whereas the idea that time is absolute suggests that time is an objective, physical phenomenon that exists independently of human consciousness.

The philosophical questions that time raises, our understanding of time has also had practical implications for the development of new technologies. For example, the development of atomic clocks and GPS systems has allowed us to make precise measurements of time, which has had a profound impact on fields such as astronomy, navigation, and communication.

It's worth noting that our understanding of time is not static, and continues to evolve as new discoveries are made and new perspectives are developed. The study of time is a multidisciplinary field that encompasses areas such as physics, mathematics, psychology, and philosophy, and the search for a comprehensive understanding of time will likely continue for many years to come.

The trajectory of our comprehension of time has been intricately woven by a myriad of influences, spanning the strides of science and technology, the tenets of philosophy and cultural ideologies, and the perennial quest for elucidation to some of humanity's most profound inquiries.

There are many fundamental questions about the nature of existence. Whether we ultimately come to a full understanding of time remains to be seen, but the journey to do so will likely be as fascinating and illuminating as it has been in the past.

The evolution of our understanding of time has been shaped by a wide range of factors, including the advances of science and technology, philosophical and cultural beliefs, and the search for answers to some of the most fundamental questions about the nature of existence. Whether we ultimately come to a full understanding of time remains to be seen, but the journey to do so will likely be as fascinating and illuminating as it has been in the past.

As our understanding of time continues to evolve, it has become increasingly clear that time is not as simple as it might seem. While we often experience time as a linear progression from the past to the present to the future, the true nature of time is much more complex and mysterious.

One of the key insights from modern physics is that time and space are intimately connected and cannot be understood independently of each other. The theory of general relativity, for example, shows that the presence of mass and energy can warp the fabric of space-time, causing time to slow down or speed up. This has been experimentally confirmed by the Global Positioning System (GPS), which has to correct for the warping of space-time in order to accurately determine the position of satellites.

Another important aspect of time is its relationship with entropy, which is a measure of the disorder in a system. According to the second law of thermodynamics, entropy in a closed system can only increase over time, leading to the concept of the "arrow of time." This arrow of time is a fundamental aspect of our experience of time, and it is thought to be related to the expansion of the universe and the increasing homogenization of energy.

Our understanding of time has been challenged by the theory of quantum mechanics, which describes the behavior of matter and energy at the smallest scales. According to quantum mechanics, particles can exist in multiple states at the same time, and their behavior is inherently probabilistic. This leads to the famous phenomenon of quantum entanglement, where particles can become correlated in such a way that a change to one particle immediately affects the other, regardless of the distance between them.

Our understanding of time has come a long way since the early days of human history, but there is still much that we don't know. As new discoveries are made and new technologies are developed, it is likely that our understanding of time will continue to evolve and expand, leading us to new insights and new questions. Regardless of what the future may hold, the study of time will likely remain one of the most fascinating and important fields of inquiry in science and philosophy.

Chapter Nine:
Time in Classical Mechanics

Classical mechanics, also known as Newtonian mechanics, is a branch of physics that studies the motion of objects under the influence of forces. In classical mechanics, time is a fundamental concept that plays a crucial role in understanding and predicting the behavior of physical systems.

In classical mechanics, time is treated as an absolute quantity that flows uniformly and independently of the physical events it measures. This means that time passes at the same rate for all observers, regardless of their relative motion or location. According to classical mechanics, time is irreversible and cannot be reversed or stopped.

In order to describe the motion of objects in classical mechanics, one needs to specify their positions and velocities at a given instant of time. The positions and velocities of objects can then be used to calculate their future positions and velocities using the laws of motion. The laws of motion, formulated by Sir Isaac Newton, state that the acceleration of an object is proportional to the net force acting on it and inversely proportional to its mass.

One of the most important implications of the concept of time in classical mechanics is the principle of causality. According to this principle, every physical event has a cause that can be traced back to earlier events in time. This means that the motion of objects can be understood as a sequence of cause-and-effect relationships, where the motion of an object at a given instant is determined by the forces acting on it and the motion of the object in the past.

In classical mechanics, time is considered as an external parameter that is independent of the physical system under consideration. This means that time is not a physical quantity that can be measured by the system, but rather a background notion that is used to describe the motion of objects. This treatment of time is in contrast to the concept of time in relativity theory, where time is treated as a physical quantity that is relative to the observer and is affected by gravity.

One of the key features of classical mechanics is its ability to make precise predictions about the motion of objects. For example, given the initial positions and velocities of objects, one can calculate their positions and velocities at any later time using the laws of motion. This makes classical mechanics a very powerful tool for making predictions about the behavior of physical systems.

Besides to its predictive capabilities, classical mechanics is also very intuitive and easy to understand. The laws of motion are simple and straightforward, and the concept of time is well-defined and easy to understand. This makes classical mechanics an ideal starting point for students learning about physics and the laws of motion.

Time plays a central role in classical mechanics and is essential for understanding and predicting the motion of physical systems. Although time is treated as an external parameter that is independent of the physical system, it allows us to make precise predictions about the motion of objects and provides a clear and intuitive understanding of the laws of motion.

In classical mechanics, time plays a crucial role in the formulation of physical laws and in the development of mathematical models that describe the motion of objects. For example, the laws of motion, which describe the motion of objects in response to forces, are formulated as differential equations that relate the position and velocity of objects to the forces acting on them and to the elapsed time.

Another important aspect of time in classical mechanics is its use in the formulation of energy concepts. Energy is a property of a physical system that is conserved over time, meaning that the total energy of a system remains constant unless acted upon by external forces. This principle of energy conservation is a cornerstone of classical mechanics and is used to predict the behavior of physical systems in a wide range of applications.

Moreover to its role in the formulation of physical laws and energy concepts, time is also used to describe the evolution of physical systems over time. For example, one can use time to describe the changes in the position and velocity of objects as they move through space, or the changes in the temperature and pressure of a gas as it expands and contracts.

It is worth noting that classical mechanics provides a foundation for the development of more advanced theories, such as quantum mechanics and special and general relativity. These theories build upon the concepts and principles of classical mechanics and provide a more complete and accurate description of the physical world at the atomic and cosmological scales.

Time is a fundamental concept in classical mechanics that plays a crucial role in the formulation of physical laws, the development of mathematical models, the description of energy and the evolution of physical systems over time. It provides a foundation for the development of more advanced theories and continues to be a topic of active research and investigation.

Chapter Ten:
Time in Relativity Theory

Relativity theory, also known as Einstein's theory of relativity, is a branch of physics that describes the behavior of physical systems in the presence of strong gravitational fields and high speeds. In contrast to classical mechanics, which treats time as an absolute and independent quantity, relativity theory treats time as a relative and physical quantity that is affected by the presence of matter and energy.

One of the key features of relativity theory is the idea of space-time, which is a four-dimensional mathematical framework that combines the three dimensions of space with the dimension of time. In this framework, the position and motion of objects are described by their coordinates in space-time, rather than just their position and velocity in space. This allows for a more comprehensive and unified description of physical systems and their interactions.

In relativity theory, time is relative to the observer and is affected by the observer's velocity, gravity, and the presence of matter and energy. This means that time passes at different rates for different observers, depending on their relative motion and location. For example, an observer moving at high speeds will experience time as passing more slowly than an observer at rest, while an observer in a strong gravitational field will experience time as passing more slowly than an observer far from any sources of gravity.

Another important aspect of time in relativity theory is its relationship to causality, which is the idea that cause and effect relationships are always preserved in the physical world. In classical mechanics, causality is based on the idea of absolute time, which flows uniformly and independently of the physical events it measures. In relativity theory, causality is based on the idea of space-time, which is curved by the presence of matter and energy. This curvature determines the direction of time and ensures that cause- and-effect relationships are preserved.

Time is a crucial and complex concept in relativity theory, which provides a more complete and accurate description of physical systems and their interactions in the presence of strong gravitational fields and high speeds. Time is treated as a relative and physical quantity that is affected by the observer's velocity, gravity, and the presence of matter and energy, and its relationship to causality is based on the idea of space-time and its curvature.

Moreover to its treatment of time, relativity theory also has a significant impact on our understanding of space. In classical mechanics, space is considered to be an absolute and unchanging framework in which objects move and interact. In contrast, relativity theory treats space as a dynamic and relative quantity that is also affected by the presence of matter and energy.

For example, in the presence of a massive object, such as a star or a planet, space is curved, and this curvature affects the motion of objects. Light, which travels in straight lines in a flat space-time, follows a curved path in the presence of a gravitational field, a phenomenon known as gravitational lensing. This effect is a key prediction of relativity theory and has been confirmed by numerous astronomical observations.

Another important aspect of space in relativity theory is the idea of black holes, which are regions of space-time where the curvature of space-time is so strong that not even light can escape. Black holes provide a fascinating and challenging test of the predictions of relativity theory and have been the subject of much research and investigation.

Time and space are central concepts in relativity theory, which provides a more complete and accurate description of physical systems and their interactions in the presence of strong gravitational fields and high speeds. Time is treated as a relative and physical quantity that is affected by the observer's velocity, gravity, and the presence of matter and energy, and its relationship to causality is based on the idea of space-time and its curvature. Space is treated as a dynamic and relative quantity that is also affected by the presence of matter and energy, and its curvature affects the motion of objects and the path of light. These concepts continue to be the subject of active research and investigation, and their implications for our understanding of the physical world are far-reaching and profound.

Relativity theory also has important implications for our understanding of the nature of energy and matter. In classical mechanics, energy and matter are considered to be separate and distinct quantities, with matter being the source of gravity and energy being the source of motion and interaction. In relativity theory, however, energy and matter are considered to be equivalent and interchangeable, and this equivalence is described by the famous equation $E=mc^2$, where E is energy, m is mass, and c is the speed of light.

This equation states that a small amount of mass can be converted into a large amount of energy, and vice versa. This idea is the basis for the development of nuclear energy and atomic bombs, and has had a profound impact on our understanding of the physical world and our ability to harness its energy.

Another important aspect of the equivalence of energy and matter is the idea of dark matter and dark energy, which are mysterious forms of matter and energy that are inferred to exist from their gravitational effects on visible matter, but have not been directly detected. Dark matter and dark energy are thought to make up most of the matter and energy in the universe, and their nature and properties continue to be a subject of active research and investigation.

Chapter Eleven:
The Nature of Time in Quantum Mechanics

In quantum mechanics, the nature of time is a topic of much debate and discussion. Unlike in classical mechanics and relativity theory, where time is treated as a continuous and absolute quantity, time in quantum mechanics is treated as a fundamentally uncertain and relative quantity.

One of the key features of quantum mechanics is the concept of wave-particle duality, which states that particles can exhibit both wave-like and particle-like behavior. This idea has important implications for the nature of time, as the wave-like behavior of particles implies that time is not a definite and continuous quantity, but is instead inherently uncertain and relative.

In quantum mechanics, the uncertainty principle states that certain pairs of physical properties, such as position and momentum, cannot both be precisely known at the same time. This uncertainty also applies to time and energy, meaning that the more precisely the energy of a system is known, the less precisely its time can be known, and vice versa.

This uncertainty in the nature of time in quantum mechanics leads to a number of interesting and challenging interpretations and implications. For example, some interpretations suggest that time is not a fundamental aspect of the universe, but is instead an emergent property that arises from the interactions of quantum systems. Others suggest that time is an absolute and continuous quantity, but that its precise value is uncertain and relative.

The nature of time in quantum mechanics is a topic of much debate and discussion, and its implications for our understanding of the physical world are far-reaching and profound. Unlike in classical mechanics and relativity theory, where time is treated as a continuous and absolute quantity, time in quantum mechanics is treated as a fundamentally uncertain and relative quantity, and its precise nature is still the subject of active research and investigation.

In quantum mechanics, the relationship between time and entropy is also an important area of study. In classical mechanics, entropy is treated as a measure of the disorder or randomness of a system, and it always increases over time. In quantum mechanics, however, entropy can remain constant or even decrease over time, suggesting that the concept of entropy may need to be modified or reinterpreted in the context of quantum mechanics.

The relationship between time and entanglement is also a topic of much discussion in quantum mechanics. Entanglement is a quantum phenomenon in which two or more particles become correlated in such a way that the state of one particle cannot be described independently of the state of the other particle, even if the particles are separated by large distances.

In some interpretations of quantum mechanics, entanglement is seen as a form of instant communication or transfer of information between particles, suggesting that time may be a relative and uncertain quantity even on the quantum level. Other interpretations suggest that entanglement is a purely statistical phenomenon that does not involve any transfer of information or communication.

The nature of time in quantum mechanics is a complex and challenging topic with far-reaching implications for our understanding of the physical world. It is treated as a fundamentally uncertain and relative quantity, and its relationship to other physical properties such as entropy and entanglement is the subject of much debate and discussion. As with many aspects of quantum mechanics, the precise nature of time remains an open question, and its interpretation and implications continue to be the subject of active research and investigation.

Also to the uncertainty and relative nature of time in quantum mechanics, there are also implications for the concept of causality, or cause and effect. In classical mechanics and relativity theory, causality is a well-defined and fundamental concept, with events being ordered in a definite cause-and-effect relationship.

In quantum mechanics, however, the uncertainty principle and the wave-like behavior of particles imply that causality is not a well-defined concept, and that the cause-and-effect relationship between events can be fundamentally uncertain. This is seen, for example, in the phenomenon of quantum entanglement, where the state of one particle can instantaneously affect the state of another particle, even if the particles are separated by large distances.

This has led to a number of interpretations of quantum mechanics that challenge traditional notions of causality and determinism, suggesting that the physical world may not be fully predictable or deterministic, and that the outcome of quantum events may be fundamentally random and indeterminate.

Chapter Twelve:
Philosophical Views on Time

Philosophers have debated the nature of time for centuries, leading to a wide range of views on this fundamental aspect of our experience. Here, we will explore some of the major philosophical perspectives on time.

Presentism: Presentism is the view that only the present exists, and the past and future are mere illusions. According to presentism, time flows continuously and the present moment is always changing. This view has been advocated by philosophers such as St. Augustine and John McTaggart.

Externalism: In contrast to presentism, externalism is the view that all points in time, past, present, and future, exist equally and simultaneously. This view has been advocated by philosophers such as Baruch Spinoza and J.M.E .Mc Taggart.

The concept of the Growing Block Universe posits that both the past and present are tangible entities, while the future remains yet to be determined, gradually emerging from the current moment. This perspective amalgamates elements of presentism and externalism and has found proponents among philosophers such as Arthur Prior and D.H. Mellor.

Process Philosophy: Process philosophy, associated with philosophers such as Alfred North Whitehead and Charles Hartshorne, holds that time is not a thing or a substance, but rather a process or a series of events. According to this view, time is not independent of the things and events that occur.

Time as a Mental Construct: Some philosophers, such as Immanuel Kant, have argued that time is a mental construct, created by the human mind to make sense of our experiences. This view holds that time is not a feature of the physical world, but rather a way of organizing and understanding it.

Philosophical views on time vary widely, from the idea that only the present exists, to the belief that all points in time exist equally, to the idea that time is a mental construct. Each of these perspectives has its own strengths and weaknesses, and the debate about the nature of time is likely to continue for many years to come.

The Block Universe Theory posits time as a fourth dimension, akin to the three spatial dimensions. Time and space are perceived as intertwined facets of a singular entity, depicting the universe as a four-dimensional block where all future events have already occurred and are statically preserved. This perspective finds support among philosophers like H.D. Lewis and C.D. Broad.

Time as a Physical Entity: Some physicists, such as Julian Barbour, have proposed that time is a physical entity that can be measured and studied. This view holds that time is not just a human invention, but a fundamental aspect of the universe that can be studied and understood through scientific investigation.

Time as Emergent: This view, advocated by philosophers such as David Lewis, holds that time is an emergent property of the physical world, rather than a fundamental aspect of it. According to this view, time arises from the interaction of physical entities and is not a separate entity in its own right.

The A-Series and the B-Series: The A-series and the B-series are two different ways of thinking about the nature of time. The A-series holds that time is dynamic and that events are ordered in terms of past, present, and future. The B-series, on the other hand, holds that events are ordered in a timeless fashion, with no reference to the present moment.

Philosophical views on time are diverse and varied, with each view offering a unique perspective on this elusive concept. Some philosophers see time as a physical entity that can be studied and understood, while others view it as a mental construct that arises from our experiences. Regardless of the view one takes, the study of time remains a fascinating and important area of philosophical inquiry.

The Moving Spotlight Theory: This view, developed by philosopher Derek Parfit, holds that the present moment is like a moving spotlight that illuminates different parts of the past, present, and future. According to this theory, the present moment is constantly changing and moving forward, but the past and future do not exist in the same way as the present.

The Open Future: This view, developed by philosophers such as John Earman and John D. Norton, holds that the future is open and indeterminate, and that our actions can influence and change the future. According to this view, the future is not fixed or determined, but is instead shaped by our choices and actions.

Time and Causality: Many philosophers have explored the relationship between time and causality, with some holding that causality is a fundamental aspect of time and that the concept of time is closely tied to the idea of cause and effect. According to this view, time is not just a way of measuring the duration of events, but is also closely tied to the way events are related to each other in a causal chain.

Philosophical views on time are diverse and complex, encompassing a wide range of perspectives and ideas. Whether one views time as a physical entity, a mental construct, or a combination of both, the study of time remains an important and fascinating area of inquiry for philosophers and scientists alike. As our understanding of the world and the universe continues to evolve, it is likely that our views on the nature of time will continue to change and evolve as well.

Chapter Thirteen:
Presentism and the A-Theory of Time

Presentism is a philosophical theory of time that holds that only the present moment is real and that the past and the future are merely imagined or nonexistent. According to presentism, the past and future are not a part of reality in the same way that the present is, and that events in the past and future do not objectively exist in the present.

The A-Theory of Time, on the other hand, asserts that time has a direction and that events occur in a linear progression from the past, through the present, and into the future. This theory maintains that time is absolute and that it flows uniformly in one direction, with the present moment being the dividing line between past and future.

The distinction between the two theories of time has important implications for our understanding of time and reality. For example, presentism implies that only what is happening right now is real, while everything that has happened in the past or will happen in the future is simply imagined or nonexistent. This view of time has implications for issues such as personal identity, causation, and the nature of change.

On the other hand, the A-Theory of Time suggests that time is objective and that events unfold in a linear progression from the past to the present to the future. This view has important implications for our understanding of causation, as it implies that events in the past and future can have a causal impact on the present.

Presentism and the A-Theory of Time are two distinct philosophical theories of time that offer different perspectives on the nature of time and reality.

Understanding these theories is important for exploring questions about the nature of time and its relationship to reality.

Additionally, both presentism and the A-Theory of Time have received support and criticism from various philosophers. Presentism has been criticized for its difficulty in accounting for the reality of the past and future, and for its implications for issues such as the persistence of objects and the nature of change.

The A-Theory of Time, on the other hand, has been criticized for its difficulties in explaining why time appears to be symmetrical and for its implications for the nature of causation. Some philosophers argue that the A-Theory of Time leads to a problematic idea of a privileged present moment, which is the only moment that is real and the only moment that can cause changes in the future.

Despite these criticisms, both presentism and the A-Theory of Time continue to be debated among philosophers, with each theory offering unique insights into the nature of time and its relationship to reality. The debate between presentism and the A-Theory of Time is likely to continue as philosophers continue to explore these fundamental questions about time and reality.

Presentism and the A-Theory of Time are two important philosophical theories of time that offer different perspectives on the nature of time and its relationship to reality. Understanding these theories is important for exploring fundamental questions about time and its role in shaping our understanding of the world.

Besides the philosophical debates surrounding presentism and the A-Theory of Time, there are also implications for other areas of inquiry, such as physics and cosmology. For example, some physicists and cosmologists have explored the implications of these theories for our understanding of the nature of time and its relationship to space and matter.

In physics, the concept of time is closely linked to the concept of space, and some physicists have explored the idea of a space-time continuum in which events are defined by their location in both space and time. This idea has important implications for our understanding of the nature of time and its relationship to space and matter, and has been central to the development of Einstein's theory of relativity.

In cosmology, the A-Theory of Time has implications for our understanding of the nature of the universe, including the origin and evolution of the cosmos. Some cosmologists have explored the idea that the universe began with a singularity, a point in the past in which all matter and energy were compressed into a tiny, dense region. From this singularity, the universe is believed to have expanded and evolved over time, following the linear progression of time as defined by the A-Theory of Time.

Presentism and the A-Theory of Time are not just important philosophical theories, but they also have implications for other areas of inquiry, including physics and cosmology. As such, they continue to be central to ongoing debates and discussions about the nature of time and its relationship to reality.

Chapter Fourteen:
The B-Theory of Time

The B-Theory of Time, also known as the "tense less theory of time," asserts that the past, present, and future are equally real and that time is simply an ordering of events in a timeline. This theory differs from the A-Theory of Time, also known as the "tensed theory of time," which claims that the present moment is the only real moment and that the past and future are merely potential.

Advocates of the B-Theory of time argue that the A-Theory of time is based on a psychological phenomenon known as "presentism," the notion that the present moment is privileged over the past and future. However, they claim that this is a subjective illusion and that there is no objective reason to consider the present as special.

According to the B-Theory, events do not change their nature as they move from the future to the past. Instead, they are simply fixed events in a four-dimensional space-time, which can be thought of as a block universe. The B-Theory also asserts that time is not flowing, but rather it is a static, unchanging entity.

One of the main arguments for the B-Theory is that it is a more parsimonious theory, as it eliminates the need for a moving present moment, which is difficult to define and explain. It also resolves the paradoxes associated with the A-Theory, such as the problem of determinism and the issue of time's direction.

Critics of the B-Theory argue that it is too abstract and removes the personal and subjective experience of time. They claim that it does not accurately capture our intuitive understanding of time and that it is unable to explain the phenomenon of temporal becoming, or the idea that events become real as they move from the future to the present.

The B-Theory of Time is a philosophical theory that asserts that the past, present, and future are equally real and that time is simply a fixed ordering of events in a timeline. While it offers a parsimonious explanation for the nature of time, it is still a matter of debate among philosophers and is opposed by those who believe in the A-Theory of Time.

The B-Theory of Time has been discussed and debated by philosophers and physicists for over a century and has had a significant impact on the study of time and space-time. One of the key figures in the development of the B-Theory was the German mathematician and philosopher, Hermann Minkowski, who introduced the concept of four-dimensional space-time in his 1908 lectures.

One of the key implications of the B-Theory is that it eliminates the concept of causality as we understand it in the A-Theory. In the B-Theory, cause and effect are simply two events that are temporally related, with one preceding the other. This has led some physicists to question the validity of the concept of causality in a space-time that is fixed and unchanging.

Another important aspect of the B-Theory is its relationship to the concept of free will. Many proponents of the B- Theory argue that if the future is just as real as the past, then the concept of free will becomes meaningless, as all future events are predetermined. This has led to a lively debate among philosophers about the nature of free will and determinism.

In recent years, the B-Theory of Time has also been discussed in the context of modern physics, particularly in the study of quantum mechanics and cosmology. Some physicists have argued that the B-Theory is more consistent with the mathematical models used in quantum mechanics and cosmology, while others argue that the A-Theory is more consistent with our everyday experience of time.

Despite its many implications, the B-Theory of Time remains a controversial theory, with many philosophers and physicists holding differing opinions about its validity. Whether it is ultimately accepted as the correct theory of time remains to be seen, but its impact on our understanding of the nature of time and space-time will likely continue to be felt for years to come.

Another philosophical debate surrounding the B-Theory concerns the relationship between time and change. Some proponents of the B-Theory argue that change is an illusion and that time is simply a collection of events that exist in a fixed and unchanging manner. Others argue that change is a real and fundamental aspect of the universe and that the B-Theory cannot adequately explain it.

The B-Theory of Time has garnered attention within the sphere of philosophy of religion, where debates ensue regarding its implications. Some philosophers contend that it aligns with a deterministic worldview, posing challenges to the notion of a personal God actively engaging with the world. Conversely, others argue for the reconciliation of the B-Theory with religious beliefs, suggesting that it does not eliminate the idea of divine intervention or the concept of freewill.

In recent years, the B-Theory of Time has gained renewed attention as a result of the development of new technologies that allow us to measure and manipulate time on a scale that was previously impossible. This has led to new questions about the nature of time and the possibility of time travel, which have both philosophical and scientific implications.

The B-Theory of Time continues to be a vibrant and important area of philosophical and scientific inquiry, with far-reaching implications for our understanding of reality and the nature of time and space-time. Whether it ultimately proves to be the correct theory of time remains to be seen, but its impact on the field of philosophy and our understanding of the world will likely continue to be felt for many years to come.

Chapter Fifteen:
The Nature of Time in Eastern Philosophy

The nature of time has been a subject of philosophical inquiry for centuries, with different cultures and traditions offering their own unique perspectives on its essence. In Eastern philosophy, time is viewed as a fluid and cyclical concept, rather than a linear progression of events.

In Hinduism, the concept of time is embodied by the deity Lord Brahma, who is said to have created the universe and all things within it. Time is seen as infinite and eternal, with each day of Brahma equaling 4.32 billion human years. The cyclical nature of time is also reflected in the Hindu concept of reincarnation, where the soul is believed to be reincarnated into different forms over countless lifetimes.

Buddhism also places a strong emphasis on the cyclical nature of time, with the doctrine of reincarnation playing a central role in the belief system. The Buddhist concept of karma dictates that a person's actions in this life will affect their experiences in future lives, creating a cycle of cause and effect that perpetuates over time. Additionally, the Buddhist belief in the impermanence of all things, including time, reinforces the idea that the present moment is always fleeting and that the future and past are constantly changing.

In Taoism, an Eastern philosophical tradition, time is perceived as an intrinsic component of the Tao, the supreme reality that encompasses the entirety of existence. Within this framework, time unfolds as a cyclical and repetitive force, wherein all phenomena within the universe adhere to a natural rhythm of emergence, expansion, deterioration, and cessation. This cyclicality finds resonance in the Taoist principle of yin and yang, where the interplay between opposing forces perpetually evolves in an unceasing cycle of transformation.

Eastern philosophy views time as a cyclical and eternal concept, with a strong emphasis on reincarnation, karma, and the impermanence of all things. Unlike Western philosophy, which tends to view time as a linear progression of events, Eastern philosophy embraces the cyclical nature of time as a fundamental aspect of the universe.

In Eastern philosophy, the nature of time is deeply intertwined with the concept of existence and the meaning of life. For example, in Hinduism, the ultimate goal of existence is to attain release from the cycle of reincarnation and merge with the ultimate reality, Brahman. In Buddhism, the goal is to achieve enlightenment and end the cycle of birth and death through the elimination of ignorance and craving.

Likewise, Eastern philosophy often views time as subjective, rather than objective, meaning that time is perceived differently by individuals based on their state of mind and level of consciousness. For example, in Zen Buddhism, time is seen as a mental construct, with the present moment being the only true reality. This idea is reflected in the Zen practice of mindfulness, which involves being fully present in the moment and letting go of thoughts about the past and future.

The cyclical nature of time also has important implications for ethics and morality in Eastern philosophy. In Hinduism, for example, a person's actions in this life will determine their experiences in future lives, leading to a focus on virtuous behavior and the avoidance of negative actions. In Buddhism, the concept of reincarnation is used to explain the interdependence of all things and the importance of treating others with compassion and kindness.

Eastern philosophy views time as a reminder of the impermanence of all things, including our own existence. This understanding leads to a focus on living in the present moment and cherishing the time we have, rather than being overly attached to material possessions or future outcomes.

Eastern philosophy offers a unique and nuanced perspective on the nature of time, viewing it as a cyclical, subjective, and interdependent concept that is deeply intertwined with existence, ethics, and the meaning of life. By embracing the cyclical nature of time and the impermanence of all things, Eastern philosophy encourages individuals to live in the present moment and cultivate virtuous behavior.

The Eastern philosophical perspective on time can also be found in the ancient Chinese philosophy of Confucianism. Confucius taught that time is valuable and should be used wisely to cultivate virtue, improve oneself, and serve others. He believed that time passes quickly and that life is short, so it is important to make the most of every moment. Confucius also taught that time is a source of change, with everything in the world undergoing a process of growth, decline, and rebirth. This cyclical understanding of time is reflected in the Confucian concept of the Mandate of Heaven, which holds that the universe operates in a cyclical pattern, with dynasties rising and falling over time.

In traditional Chinese medicine, the concept of time is also an important aspect of healing. In this system, the flow of energy in the body is believed to follow a circadian rhythm, with each organ having a two-hour period of maximum energy. Practitioners of traditional Chinese medicine use this understanding of time to diagnose and treat illnesses, taking into account the body's natural rhythms and the cyclical nature of health and illness.

The cyclical view of time in Eastern philosophy also has implications for aesthetics and art. For example, in traditional Japanese arts such as flower arrangement, calligraphy, and the tea ceremony, the arrangement of objects and the timing of actions are considered to be as important as their appearance. These arts emphasize the importance of being fully present in the moment and living in harmony with the natural rhythms of the universe.

Eastern philosophy offers a rich and diverse perspective on the nature of time, encompassing a wide range of beliefs and practices that are deeply rooted in the cultures and traditions of the region. From the emphasis on living in the present moment in Zen Buddhism, to the importance of wise use of time in Confucianism, to the use of the cyclical nature of time in traditional Chinese medicine, Eastern philosophy offers a unique and insightful perspective on this complex and multifaceted concept.

Chapter Sixteen:
Time and the Mind

Time stands as a beguiling enigma that has captivated the minds of philosophers, scientists, and theologians across epochs. While regarded as a fundamental aspect of reality, its elusive nature renders it one of the most challenging concepts to grasp fully. The intricate relationship between time and the human psyche adds another layer of complexity, remaining largely elusive.

From a psychological standpoint, time manifests differently within the confines of the mind compared to its objective existence in the physical realm. Subjectivity characterizes the experience of time, with events perceived to unfold at varying speeds contingent upon an individual's mental disposition, age, and cultural context. For instance, instances of heightened excitement or stress can seemingly stretch time, elongating moments, while the passage of time accelerates with age.

Furthermore, the brain's limited capacity to process information plays a pivotal role in shaping our perception of time. As the cognitive load increases, time appears to decelerate, manifesting in instances where time appears to drag during monotonous activities or lengthy meetings. Conversely, when fully engrossed in stimulating endeavors, time appears to warp, seemingly accelerating its space.

Additionally, the mind has the ability to manipulate time through various mental strategies such as mindfulness, self-reflection, and memory recall. When people engage in these activities, they are able to slow down their perception of time and live in the moment. This can help to increase feelings of happiness, contentment, and well-being.

The relationship between time and the mind is a complex and multifaceted one. Time is experienced differently by the mind than it is by physical reality, and the mind has the ability to manipulate time through various mental strategies. Understanding this relationship can help people to better appreciate and make the most of their time, as well as improve their overall mental health and well-being.

Furthermore, time also plays an important role in our mental development and growth. The passage of time allows for new experiences, the formation of memories, and the evolution of our thoughts, beliefs, and values. Our experiences shape our understanding of time, and as our understanding of time evolves, so too does our understanding of the world around us.

Moreover, the concept of time can also have a profound impact on our sense of self. Our sense of self is tied to our memories, and the memories that we have of our past experiences shape our sense of self and our identity. As time passes, our memories and experiences accumulate, and our sense of self evolves and becomes more complex.

Also, time is a crucial aspect of mental health and well-being. The passage of time can bring new opportunities, but it can also lead to loss and change. The way we handle and cope with these changes can greatly impact our mental health and well-being. For example, people who are able to adapt to change and find meaning in their experiences are more likely to have better mental health than those who struggle to cope with change.

The relationship between time and the mind is a complex and dynamic one. Time is experienced differently by the mind, and the mind has the ability to manipulate time through various mental strategies. Time also plays a crucial role in our mental development and growth, our sense of self, and our mental health and well-being. It is important to be mindful of the role that time plays in our lives and to take steps to make the most of our time and to maintain our mental health and well-being.

It is also important to note that the concept of time is culturally relative and can vary across different societies and cultures. For example, some indigenous cultures have a more cyclical understanding of time, where events and experiences repeat in a pattern. Western cultures, on the other hand, tend to view time as linear, with events moving forward in a straightforward manner. These differing cultural views of time can impact the way people understand and experience the world around them, as well as their mental health and well-being.

Additionally, the experience of time can also be influenced by individual differences such as personality and temperament. For example, people who are naturally more spontaneous and impulsive may experience time as moving more quickly, while those who are more structured and organized may experience time as moving more slowly. These individual differences can impact the way people approach time and how they prioritize their time and experiences.

It is important to consider the role that technology plays in our perception of time. In today's fast-paced and technologically advanced world, people are constantly connected and bombarded with information. This can lead to feelings of overstimulation and a sense of time moving more quickly. It is important to take breaks from technology and to engage in activities that allow for a slower and more mindful experience of time.

The relationship between time and the mind is a complex and multifaceted one that is influenced by a variety of factors including culture, individual differences, and technology. Understanding the role that time plays in our lives can help us to make the most of our time, prioritize our experiences, and maintain our mental health and well- being.

Chapter Seventeen:
The Subjective Experience of Time

Time is a fundamental aspect of our reality, yet it is also one of the most elusive and difficult to define. While scientists can measure time objectively using clocks and calendars, the subjective experience of time is much more complex and varies from person to person.

One of the key ways that people experience time subjectively is through their perception of its speed. For example, time can seem to fly by when we are having fun or engaged in an interesting activity, while it can drag on when we are bored or in a situation we find unpleasant. This subjective experience of time is influenced by a variety of factors, including our mental state, emotions, and attention.

Another aspect of the subjective experience of time is memory. Memories are integral to our sense of self and our understanding of time, and the way we recall memories can have a significant impact on our perception of time. For example, people often remember events from their childhood as happening much longer ago than they actually did, which can give the impression that time has flown by.

Besides these factors, the subjective experience of time can also be influenced by individual differences such as personality and temperament. For example, people who are naturally more organized and structured may experience time as moving more slowly, while those who are more spontaneous and impulsive may experience it as moving more quickly.

Moreover, cultural differences can also play a role in the subjective experience of time. Different cultures have different views and understandings of time, which can impact the way people prioritize their experiences and the importance they place on the passage of time.

The subjective experience of time is a complex and multifaceted phenomenon that is influenced by a variety of factors, including mental state, emotions, attention, memory, individual differences, and cultural background. Understanding the subjective experience of time can help people to appreciate and make the most of their time, as well as improve their overall well-being and quality of life.

One interesting aspect of the subjective experience of time is the phenomenon of temporal illusions. Temporal illusions are instances where our perception of time does not match objective reality. For example, people often report that time seems to slow down during high-stress or high-stakes situations, such as a car accident or a dangerous experience. This phenomenon is known as time dilation and is thought to be a result of the way that the brain processes information during these types of situations.

Another example of a temporal illusion is the paradoxical experience of time when traveling. People often report that time seems to move more quickly when they are on vacation or traveling, even though they are technically experiencing more events and activities than they would at home. This phenomenon is thought to be due to the fact that our brains are processing more new and novel information, which gives the impression that time is moving more quickly.

Additionally, the subjective experience of time can also be influenced by drugs and substances. For example, people who use psychedelics such as LSD or psilocybin often report experiencing a distorted sense of time, with time seeming to slow down or speed up. Similarly, people who use stimulants such as caffeine or cocaine may experience time as moving more quickly.

The subjective experience of time is a fascinating and complex phenomenon that is influenced by a variety of internal and external factors. From temporal illusions and the impact of stress and novelty, to the effects of drugs and substances, the way that people experience time is a unique and personal aspect of the human experience.

Understanding the subjective experience of time can help people to appreciate and make the most of their time, and to better understand the complexities of the human mind and perception.

It is important to consider the impact of mindfulness and meditation on the subjective experience of time. Mindfulness and meditation are practices that focus on paying attention to the present moment and being aware of one's thoughts and feelings. This focus on the present moment can help to slow down the subjective experience of time and increase a sense of peace and well-being.

Research has shown that mindfulness and meditation can have a positive impact on mental health, reducing symptoms of anxiety and depression and increasing feelings of happiness and contentment. Additionally, these practices can help to improve attention and focus, reducing distractions and allowing for a more enjoyable and productive experience of time.

The subjective experience of time is a complex and multifaceted phenomenon that is influenced by a variety of internal and external factors. From temporal illusions and the impact of stress and novelty, to the effects of drugs and substances and the benefits of mindfulness and meditation, the way that people experience time is a unique and personal aspect of the human experience. Understanding the subjective experience of time and how to manage it can help people to appreciate and make the most of their time, and to improve their overall well-being and quality of life.

Chapter Eighteen:
Time Perception and the Brain

Time perception is a complex process that is influenced by a variety of factors, including our biology, environment, and personal experiences. The brain plays a central role in our experience of time, as it is responsible for processing and integrating information from a wide range of sensory inputs to create a coherent sense of the passage of time.

One of the key structures involved in time perception is the supra-chiasmatic nucleus (SCN), located in the hypothalamus of the brain. The SCN acts as the brain's "biological clock", regulating the circadian rhythms that govern our sleep-wake cycle and other physiological processes. The SCN receives information about light and dark from the eyes, which helps to set and reset the body's internal clock.

Another important structure involved in time perception is the basal ganglia, which is a group of nuclei in the brain that play a role in motor control, habit formation, and other functions. The basal ganglia have been found to be involved in the experience of duration, as well as the perception of rhythm and pattern.

The cerebellum, a structure located at the base of the brain, is also thought to play a role in time perception. The cerebellum is involved in motor control and coordination, and has been found to be involved in the perception of time intervals in the range of hundreds of milliseconds to several seconds.

The parietal cortex, located in the brain's lateral sulcus, is also involved in time perception. The parietal cortex receives sensory information from various parts of the body and is involved in processing information about space and time. It has been found to be involved in the perception of both short-term and long-term intervals.

Time perception is a complex process that involves the integration of information from a wide range of sensory inputs by various structures in the brain. From the suprachiasmatic nucleus, which regulates circadian rhythms and sets the body's internal clock, to the basal ganglia, cerebellum, and parietal cortex, which are involved in the perception of duration and time intervals, the brain plays a central role in our experience of the passage of time.

Understanding the mechanisms of time perception in the brain can help to shed light on the intricacies of the human mind and perception.

Another important aspect of time perception and the brain is the role of attention. Attention is a limited resource, and the more we focus on a particular task or activity, the more time seems to slow down. This phenomenon is known as time compression and is thought to be a result of the increased processing of information that occurs when our attention is focused.

Stress and emotions also play a role in time perception. During stressful or emotionally charged events, time seems to slow down as our brain focuses on processing the information and stimuli related to the event. This phenomenon is known as time dilation and is thought to be a survival mechanism that helps us respond more effectively to dangerous or important situations.

It is important to consider the impact of aging on time perception and the brain. As we age, our ability to process information and make decisions decreases, which can result in a slower subjective experience of time. Additionally, changes in the brain that occur with aging can also impact time perception, leading to differences in the experience of time across the lifespan.

Time perception is a complex and multifaceted process that is influenced by various factors, including the brain, attention, stress and emotions, and aging. Understanding the ways in which these factors impact time perception can help to shed light on the intricacies of the human mind and perception, and to better understand the subjective experience of time.

Time perception is a complex and multifaceted phenomenon that is largely shaped by the activity of various regions in the brain. Despite the fact that time is a fundamental aspect of our experience and a crucial aspect of our daily lives, the mechanisms by which the brain perceives and processes time are not yet fully understood.

The perception of time can be influenced by various factors, including attention, emotion, and prior knowledge. For example, when we are highly focused on a task, time seems to fly by, while when we are bored, time seems to drag. Similarly, when we are anxious or excited, time seems to slow down. Additionally, our prior knowledge of how long an event should last can also influence our perception of time.

Time perception is a complex and multi-layered phenomenon that is shaped by the activity of several regions in the brain, including the supra-chiasmatic nucleus, basal ganglia, parietal cortex, and prefrontal cortex. While much remains to be discovered about the mechanisms of time perception, it is clear that it is influenced by a variety of factors, including attention, emotion, and prior knowledge.

Chapter Nineteen:
The Relationship Between Time and Consciousness

The relationship between time and consciousness is a topic that has long been debated by philosophers, scientists, and researchers. While time is a seemingly objective concept that can be measured and quantified, consciousness is a subjective experience that is unique to each individual. Despite this, there is evidence to suggest that the two are deeply interconnected, with time playing a crucial role in shaping our perception of reality.

One of the key ways in which time influences our consciousness is through its effect on memory. Our memories are constructed through the repeated activation of neural networks in the brain, with the passage of time serving to reinforce these connections. This helps us to remember past events, and gives us a sense of continuity and progression as we move through life. At the same time, our perception of time is constantly being shaped by the events that we experience, with certain moments standing out more vividly in our memories due to their emotional significance.

Anticipation of the future influences how we perceive ourselves in the present moment. Time provides the framework within which we contextualize our identity, allowing us to reflect on past events and project ourselves into future scenarios. Our memories, which are inherently tied to time, play a crucial role in constructing our sense of self by providing a narrative through which we interpret our experiences and form coherent identities.

Moreover, our perception of time can influence our sense of self in various ways. For instance, individuals who perceive time as abundant may approach life with a sense of leisure and opportunity, shaping their identity around exploration and growth. On the other hand, those who perceive time as scarce may feel pressured to achieve certain milestones within specific deadlines, leading to a more goal-oriented or achievement-focused sense of self.

Additionally, cultural and societal factors also play a significant role in shaping our perception of time and, consequently, our sense of self. Different cultures may have distinct temporal orientations, emphasizing either past traditions, present experiences, or future aspirations, which can profoundly influence individuals' identities within those cultural contexts.

In essence, time serves as a fundamental dimension through which we construct and understand our sense of self. Our memories, experiences, and cultural influences interact with our perception of time to shape our identities, highlighting the intricate relationship between time and consciousness.

The relationship between time and consciousness can also be explored in terms of the concept of mindfulness. Mindfulness is a state of awareness in which we are fully present in the moment, and it has been shown to have a number of benefits for our mental health and wellbeing. By focusing on the present moment, we are able to gain a deeper understanding of our thoughts, feelings, and experiences, and this can help us to develop a more stable sense of self over time.

The relationship between time and consciousness is a complex and multifaceted one, with time playing a crucial role in shaping our perception of reality. Whether through its impact on memory, sense of self, or mindfulness, time is an integral part of our conscious experience, and a deeper understanding of this relationship has the potential to unlock new insights into the nature of both time and consciousness.

It is also worth mentioning that the relationship between time and consciousness is not just limited to the individual level. Time also plays a crucial role in shaping our collective consciousness, and has a profound impact on the ways in which societies develop and change over time.

For example, the passage of time can shape our collective beliefs, values, and norms, as well as our understanding of history and cultural heritage. This has a significant impact on our collective sense of identity, and can contribute to the development of shared cultural narratives that help to bind people together.

Time also influences the way in which we think about the future. Our perception of the future is shaped by our experiences and expectations, and this in turn influences the choices that we make and the actions that we take. This is particularly relevant in the context of social and political issues, where our collective vision of the future can play a major role in shaping policy decisions and shaping the direction of society as a whole.

The relationship between time and consciousness is a rich and complex field of study, with far-reaching implications for our understanding of human behavior and experience. Whether at the individual or collective level, time plays a crucial role in shaping our perceptions of reality and our sense of self, and a deeper understanding of this relationship has the potential to inform our approach to a wide range of important issues.

Moreover, the concept of time is also closely tied to our experience of consciousness in terms of the concept of time perception. Time perception refers to our subjective experience of the passage of time, and it is influenced by a variety of factors, including attention, memory, and emotion.

For example, our perception of time can seem to slow down or speed up depending on the level of attention and focus we are giving to a particular task or event. This is why time seems to fly by when we are engaged in an enjoyable activity, but drag on when we are bored or in a state of stress.

Emotions also play a key role in shaping our perception of time. Positive emotions tend to make time seem to pass more quickly, while negative emotions can make it seem to slow down. This is because emotions can affect our level of attention and focus, and they also influence the ways in which we process and remember events.

The relationship between time and consciousness can also be explored in terms of the concept of temporal illusion. Temporal illusion refers to the phenomenon in which our perception of time is distorted by the context in which it is experienced. For example, time can seem to drag on when we are in a state of boredom or anxiety, but can seem to pass quickly when we are in a state of flow or focused attention.

The relationship between time and consciousness is a complex and multifaceted one, and a deeper understanding of this relationship has the potential to shed light on a wide range of important questions, including our perception of the passage of time, the role of attention and emotion in shaping our experience of time, and the ways in which time influences our sense of self and our collective consciousness.

Chapter Twenty:
Time in Culture and Society

Time is a central concept in culture and society, playing a critical role in shaping our experiences and determining how we live our lives. Whether it's the ticking of a clock, the changing of the seasons, or the rhythms of daily life, time is woven into the fabric of human society.

In many cultures, time is seen as a valuable resource, something to be managed and used wisely. This is reflected in the saying, "Time is money," which highlights the connection between time and financial success. People often feel pressure to use their time efficiently, to maximize productivity, and to achieve their goals.

This emphasis on efficiency and productivity is particularly evident in modern societies, where people are constantly on the go and there seems to be no time to waste. The fast pace of life and the rapid advance of technology have created a world that values speed and efficiency, leading people to feel like they are always in a rush.

However, not all cultures see time in the same way. In some cultures, time is viewed as a more fluid concept, with less emphasis on punctuality and more emphasis on relationships and social connections. In these cultures, it's not uncommon for people to take their time, savoring the moment, and enjoying life's simple pleasures.

This difference in views of time is often reflected in different attitudes toward work and leisure. In societies that value efficiency and productivity, work is seen as a central part of life, and people are expected to work long hours and prioritize their careers. In contrast, cultures that emphasize relationships and social connections tend to value leisure time and prioritize time with friends and family.

Time also has a profound impact on our sense of identity and belonging. Our experiences, memories, and personal relationships are all tied to time, helping us to create a sense of self and place in the world. Time can also be a source of stress and anxiety, as people worry about the future and fear they will not have enough time to achieve their goals.

Time is a complex and multifaceted concept that plays a critical role in shaping our experiences and determining how we live our lives. From the way we view work and leisure, to the relationships and memories we create, time is an essential part of who we are and the societies in which we live.

Besides its impact on individuals, time also has a significant influence on society as a whole. From the development of civilization and the formation of nations, to the creation of laws and social norms, time has played a crucial role in shaping the world we live in today.

One of the most significant examples of this is the way that time has shaped our calendars and timekeeping systems. The Gregorian calendar, for example, is used by most of the world today, and is based on astronomical observations and the cycles of the sun and moon. This system provides a shared sense of time that helps to bring people together and facilitate communication and trade.

In terms of law and social norms, time can also play an important role. For example, in many cultures, punctuality is seen as a sign of respect and professionalism, and people who are late are often seen as unreliable. This can impact everything from personal relationships to business dealings, and has a significant impact on the functioning of society as a whole.

Time is an integral part of culture and society, affecting our experiences and shaping the world we live in. Whether it's the way we view work and leisure, the relationships we form, or the way society functions as a whole, time is a powerful and pervasive force that influences every aspect of our lives.

Time is also closely tied to our beliefs, values, and traditions. In many cultures, religious and spiritual rituals are tied to the passage of time, such as daily prayers, weekly worship services, or annual holidays. These rituals serve to anchor people in time, helping to give their lives meaning and structure, and providing a sense of community and belonging.

For example, the celebration of holidays like Christmas and Easter, which mark important events in the Christian calendar, bring people together, fostering a sense of community and shared history. Similarly, the observance of religious holidays like Ramadan, Diwali, and Hanukkah, can serve to unite people from different backgrounds, helping to promote understanding and respect between different cultures and communities.

Moreover, time is also tied to our sense of history and legacy. Throughout history, people have sought to commemorate important events and the lives of their ancestors, creating a sense of continuity and a connection to the past. This is reflected in monuments, museums, and other institutions that preserve the history and cultural heritage of a community or nation.

Time is a complex and powerful concept that plays a critical role in shaping our experiences, beliefs, and values.

From our relationships and personal identities, to the way society functions and our shared cultural heritage, time influences every aspect of our lives and the world we live in. Understanding its impact and the different ways in which it is perceived and valued by different cultures is essential for promoting understanding, respect, and cooperation between people and communities.

Chapter Twenty-One:
Time and its Impact on Human Behavior and Society

Time is a ubiquitous and inescapable part of our lives, shaping our experiences and influencing our behavior in countless ways. From the way we manage our days and plan for the future, to the relationships we form and the memories we create, time has a profound impact on human behavior and society.

One of the most significant impacts of time on human behavior is the way it affects our perception of urgency and importance. When time is limited, people often feel a sense of urgency, which can drive them to prioritize their goals and make quick decisions. This can have both positive and negative effects, as people may become more productive and focused, but also risk making impulsive or poorly thought-out choices.

In terms of society, time plays a critical role in shaping our values, beliefs, and norms. For example, the importance placed on punctuality in many cultures can affect everything from personal relationships to business dealings. Being late is often seen as a sign of disrespect, while being prompt and reliable is valued as a sign of professionalism and dependability.

Furthermore, time is also closely tied to our sense of identity and personal history. Our experiences and memories are all tied to the passage of time, helping us to create a sense of self and a connection to the world around us. This can have a profound impact on our sense of belonging and well-being, as well as our relationships with others.

In terms of broader societal impact, time can also play a role in shaping economic systems and labor practices. For example, the development of the industrial revolution and the growth of capitalism has been closely tied to the way time is managed and perceived in modern societies. The focus on efficiency and productivity has led to a fast-paced and often stressful work environment, where people are expected to balance multiple demands and responsibilities.

Time is a central concept in human behavior and society, shaping our experiences, values, and beliefs in countless ways. Whether it's the way we perceive urgency and importance, our sense of identity and personal history, or the functioning of broader societal systems, time has a profound impact on the world we live in. Understanding its influence and the different ways in which it is perceived and valued by different cultures and societies is essential for promoting well-being, understanding, and cooperation between individuals and communities.

Besides its impact on individuals and society, time also has a significant impact on our mental and emotional health. The constant pressure to meet deadlines and manage multiple responsibilities can lead to feelings of stress and burnout, while the fast-paced and ever-changing nature of modern life can leave people feeling overwhelmed and disconnected.

Moreover, our relationship with time can also influence our sense of purpose and satisfaction in life. For example, people who feel like they never have enough time to do the things they want to do may experience feelings of frustration and unhappiness, while those who have a strong sense of control over their time often report higher levels of well-being and satisfaction.

Another important impact of time on society is the way it affects our sense of community and belonging. In many cultures, rituals and traditions that are tied to the passage of time serve to bring people together, fostering a sense of shared history and identity. For example, the celebration of holidays, religious observances, and other important events can serve to unite people from different backgrounds and help to promote understanding and respect between different communities.

Time can also have a significant impact on the environment. The fast-paced and resource-intensive nature of modern life has led to environmental degradation and the depletion of natural resources, putting our planet and its inhabitants at risk. This highlights the importance of considering our relationship with time and the impact it has on the world around us, and the need to develop more sustainable and environmentally conscious approaches to the way we live and work.

Time has a profound impact on human behavior, society, and the world around us. From our mental and emotional health, to our sense of purpose and community, to the health of the planet, time influences every aspect of our lives and the world we live in. By understanding its impact and developing more mindful and sustainable approaches to the way we use our time, we can promote well-being, understanding, and cooperation between individuals and communities, and help to build a better world for future generations.

It's worth noting that our understanding and perception of time can also vary greatly across cultures and societies. For example, in some cultures, time is seen as a strict and unyielding force that must be adhered to, while in others, it is viewed as more flexible and open to interpretation. In some cases, this can lead to misunderstandings and cultural conflicts, as people from different backgrounds have different expectations and norms around time.

Additionally, our relationship with time can also be shaped by technology and the tools we use to manage it. For example, the widespread use of computers, smartphones, and other digital devices has had a profound impact on the way people interact with time. On the one hand, technology has made it easier for people to stay connected and manage their time more efficiently, but on the other hand, it has also increased the pressure to be constantly available and respond to demands in real-time.

Another impact of technology on time is the way it has altered our sense of pace and the pace of life itself. The fast-paced and ever-changing nature of the digital age has led to a rapid acceleration of time, where events and experiences happen at a breakneck speed, and it can be difficult to keep up. This can have a significant impact on our mental and emotional health, leaving us feeling overwhelmed and stressed.

The impact of time on human behavior and society is complex and multifaceted, influenced by a wide range of factors, including culture, technology, and individual experience. By continuing to explore and understand these relationships, we can work to promote more positive and sustainable approaches to the way we live and interact with time, and build stronger and more resilient communities and societies.

Chapter Twenty-Two:
Time as a Cultural Construct

Time is often perceived as an absolute and universal concept, but in reality, it is a culturally constructed phenomenon. Different cultures have their own unique perceptions of time and its role in their lives. The way people experience, measure, and value time can vary greatly from one culture to another.

In Western cultures, time is typically seen as linear, with a clear beginning, middle, and end. People in these cultures often place a high value on punctuality and keeping to a schedule. In contrast, many indigenous cultures view time as cyclical, with events repeating themselves in a never- ending cycle. These cultures may place a greater emphasis on living in the moment and being present in the here and now.

Another example of cultural differences in time perception is the use of time in work and business. In Western cultures, time is often viewed as a scarce and valuable resource that must be managed efficiently. Business meetings, for example, are often tightly scheduled and focused on maximizing productivity. In contrast, many cultures in Latin America and the Caribbean have a more relaxed attitude toward time, with meetings often starting later than scheduled and taking longer than planned.

The way time is represented and communicated is also culturally influenced. In Western cultures, time is often communicated using digital or analog clocks, and expressed in units such as hours, minutes, and seconds. In many indigenous cultures, time is communicated through the use of calendars, with specific dates and events marking important times of the year.

Time is not a universal concept, but a culturally constructed one. Different cultures have their own unique perceptions of time and its role in their lives, and this is reflected in the way time is experienced, measured, and valued. Understanding these cultural differences can help us to better appreciate and respect the diverse perspectives on time that exist around theworld.

Time is a concept that is central to human culture and experience, yet it is not a tangible or objective reality. Rather, time is a cultural construct, meaning that its meaning and understanding are shaped by the values, beliefs, and practices of a particular society.

In many cultures, time is seen as a linear progression from the past, through the present, to the future. This view of time is closely tied to the idea of causality, where events in the past lead inevitably to events in the present and future. This linear view of time is often closely tied to the idea of progress, with the belief that society is constantly moving forward and improving.

However, not all cultures view time in this way. Some indigenous cultures, for example, have a more cyclical understanding of time, where the past and future are seen as interconnected and the present is seen as a repetition of patterns that have occurred before. This view of time is often tied to a spiritual or religious understanding, where time is seen as a cycle of birth, death, and rebirth.

Time is also a cultural construct in the sense that the way it is measured and experienced can vary greatly between cultures. For example, some cultures divide the day into 24 equal hours, while others divide it into 12 or more unequal parts. Similarly, the way in which time is represented, such as with clocks and calendars, can also vary between cultures.

The cultural meaning of time can also change over time. For example, in the past, time was often seen as a precious and limited resource, and it was important to use it wisely. Today, in many cultures, time is often seen as a commodity that can be bought and sold, with the rise of the "time is money "mentality.

Time is not an objective reality, but a cultural construct that is shaped by the beliefs, values, and practices of a particular society. Understanding time as a cultural construct is important for appreciating the diversity of human experience and the way in which different cultures understand and experience time differently.

It is also important to note that time can have different meanings and purposes in different contexts. For example, in a business setting, time may be viewed as a resource to be managed and optimized in order to maximize productivity and profits. In a religious or spiritual context, time may be seen as a way to connect with a higher power or to gain a deeper understanding of one's place in the world.

Moreover, time is not only a cultural construct but it also has a significant impact on culture and society. The way in which time is experienced and understood can shape social norms, behavior, and attitudes. For example, the emphasis on punctuality in some cultures can reflect a strong value placed on efficiency and organization, while in others, a more relaxed attitude towards time can reflect a greater emphasis on relationships and community.

The cultural construction of time can also impact individual experiences and well-being. For example, in cultures that place a high value on punctuality, individuals who frequently arrive late may experience feelings of shame or guilt, while in cultures where a more relaxed attitude towards time prevails, this may not be the case.

It is worth mentioning that the experience of time is not static, but can change and evolve over time. For example, advances in technology and transportation have allowed people to experience time in new ways, with the ability to move quickly from one place to another and to keep track of time with greater accuracy. As society and technology continue to change, so too will the experience and understanding of time.

Time is not just a concept, but a complex and dynamic cultural construct that has a significant impact on culture, society, and individuals. Recognizing the cultural construction of time can help us to better understand the diversity of human experiences and the way in which our experiences of time shape and are shaped by our culture and society.

Chapter Twenty-Three:
The Relationship Between Time and Technology

The relationship between time and technology is complex and dynamic, with technology playing a significant role in shaping our experiences and understandings of time. Technology has revolutionized the way in which we measure, experience, and manage time, and has had a profound impact on our culture and society.

One of the most significant ways in which technology has changed our relationship with time is through the development of precise and accurate timekeeping devices, such as clocks and calendars. The invention of the mechanical clock in the 14th century marked a turning point in the history of timekeeping, allowing for greater accuracy and precision in the measurement of time. The development of the quartz clock and digital clock in the 20th century further improved the accuracy and precision of timekeeping, making it possible to measure time to the fraction of a second.

Technology has also transformed the way in which we experience time. Advances in transportation and communication have made it possible to move quickly from one place to another and to keep in touch with people across vast distances. The rise of the internet and digital devices has further changed the way in which we experience time, with the ability to access information and communicate with others instantaneously. These changes have altered our relationship with time, making it possible to experience time in new and different ways.

Technology has had a significant impact on the way in which we manage time. The widespread use of technology in the workplace, for example, has made it possible to be productive and efficient, allowing us to complete tasks in less time. At the same time, technology has also introduced new distractions and demands on our time, leading to feelings of stress and burnout.

Technology has also played a role in changing the cultural meanings and understandings of time. For example, the emphasis on efficiency and productivity in many cultures can be traced back to the rise of the industrial revolution and the development of technology that allowed for greater efficiency in production. Similarly, the rise of the "time is money" mentality can be seen as a reflection of the increasing importance of technology and economic progress in our culture.

Indeed, the impact of technology on our relationship with time is profound and multifaceted, but it's crucial to recognize that technology is not neutral. The design, development, and utilization of technology are deeply embedded within social, cultural, and economic contexts, and they can both reflect and perpetuate existing power dynamics and inequalities.

One significant aspect of this dynamic is the digital divide, which refers to the gap between those who have access to digital technologies and those who do not. This gap can manifest along various dimensions, including socioeconomic status, geography, age, and education level. Those who have access to technology often enjoy advantages in terms of communication, information access, and productivity, which can lead to greater freedoms and opportunities. Conversely, those without access may face barriers to participation in the digital age, further widening existing inequalities.

Furthermore, the design choices made in the development of technology can also influence our relationship with time and exacerbate inequalities. For example, algorithms used in social media platforms or online services may prioritize certain content or users based on factors such as popularity or advertising revenue, shaping users' experiences of time spent online and potentially reinforcing existing biases or discrimination.

Moreover, the pervasive nature of technology in modern society means that it can influence how we perceive and value time. The constant connectivity facilitated by smartphones and the internet has blurred the boundaries between work and leisure time, leading to phenomena such as "always-on" culture and increased expectations for immediate responsiveness. This can contribute to feelings of time pressure and stress, particularly for those who are unable to disconnect due to economic or social pressures.

In summary, while technology has undoubtedly revolutionized our relationship with time in many ways, it's essential to acknowledge that it is not a neutral force. The unequal distribution of technology access and the design choices made in its development can perpetuate existing inequalities and shape our experiences of time in complex and often unequal ways. Recognizing these dynamics is crucial for addressing the societal implications of technological advancement and working towards a more equitable future.

Moreover, technology has also raised ethical questions about the way in which we use our time. The rise of social media and digital devices, for example, has led to concerns about screen time and the impact of technology on our well-being. The temptation to constantly check our devices and be connected to the internet can lead to feelings of stress and burnout, and can also have negative impacts on our relationships and mental health.

The relationship between time and technology is complex and ever-evolving, and requires careful consideration of the ethical and social implications of technology. While technology has greatly impacted our relationship with time and has many benefits, it is important to recognize the potential consequences and to use technology in a responsible and sustainable way. By doing so, we can ensure that technology enhances, rather than detracts from, our experiences and understanding of time.

It's also worth noting that technology has changed our perceptions of time in many different ways. For instance, instant gratification has become a norm, with the ability to receive information and communicate with others in real-time. This has also led to an increased expectation for immediate response and resolution of issues, which can be both a benefit and a challenge.

Furthermore, technology has also changed our sense of temporality, or the way in which we understand and experience the passage of time. The idea of "present shock," for example, describes the disorienting experience of living in a world where information is constantly changing and updates are happening in real-time. This can lead to feelings of overwhelm and a sense of not being able to keep up with the pace of change.

Moreover, technology has also changed the way in which we use time, and our relationship with time. The rise of the gig economy, for example, has led to a flexible and nontraditional work schedule, with people working from home, in coffee shops, and on the go. This has challenged traditional ideas of work-life balance, and has made it more difficult for people to separate their work and personal time.

Technology has had a profound impact on our relationship with time, and continues to shape and change our experiences and understandings of time in complex and multifaceted ways. It is important to be aware of these changes, and to critically examine the impacts of technology on our relationship with time, in order to ensure that we are using technology in a way that enhances our well-being and supports our values and goals.

Chapter Twenty-Four:
The Current State of Understanding the Nature of Time

The concept of time is central to our understanding of the universe, yet it remains one of the most mysterious and elusive aspects of physics. Despite centuries of study and experimentation, the nature of time is still not fully understood, and it continues to be the subject of much debate and research.

One of the biggest challenges in understanding time is that it is both a physical and a perceptual phenomenon. On the one hand, time can be measured and described in terms of the physical laws that govern the universe, such as the flow of energy and matter. On the other hand, time is also subjective and perceived differently by individuals, depending on factors such as age, culture, and experience.

One of the main areas of research in the study of time is the relationship between time and space. In the theory of general relativity, developed by Albert Einstein, time and space are considered to be intertwined and dependent on each other. According to this theory, time is not a universal constant, but instead is relative to the observer and can be affected by the presence of matter and energy.

Another important aspect of time is its directionality, or the fact that time always seems to move forward. This idea is known as the "arrow of time," and it is still not fully understood why time moves in only one direction. Some physicists believe that the arrow of time is related to the increase in entropy, or disorder, in the universe, while others have proposed that it may be a fundamental aspect of the universe that cannot be explained by any physical laws.

In recent years, there has been increased interest in the relationship between time and quantum mechanics, the theory that describes the behavior of matter and energy on a microscopic level. Some physicists believe that a better understanding of the quantum nature of time could help to reconcile the differences between general relativity and quantum mechanics and lead to a unified theory of physics.

However, despite these advances, the nature of time remains one of the greatest mysteries in physics, and it is likely that it will continue to be a subject of research and speculation for many years to come. Some physicists and philosophers even argue that it may be impossible for us to fully understand time, given the limitations of our current knowledge and our ability to perceive the world around us.

The current state of understanding the nature of time is still in its early stages, and much more research is needed to fully understand this complex and multifaceted concept. However, the ongoing research and advancements in this field have the potential to deepen our understanding of the universe and lead to new insights into the nature of reality. Whether time will ever be fully understood remains to be seen, but it is certain that the study of time will continue to be a central and fascinating area of inquiry for generations to come.

Another recent development in the study of time is the exploration of the concept of time in different cultures and historical periods. It has been found that different cultures have developed different interpretations and understandings of time, reflecting the social, economic, and political conditions of the time. For example, some ancient cultures saw time as cyclical, with events repeating themselves in regular patterns, while others saw time as linear, with a clear beginning and end.

This research highlights the importance of culture and the historical context in our understanding of time, and the need for a more interdisciplinary approach to studying time. By considering the cultural, historical, and philosophical dimensions of time, we can gain a more nuanced and complete understanding of this fundamental concept.

Another area of interest in the study of time is the psychological aspect of time perception. It has been found that people's perception of time can be affected by various factors, such as attention, emotion, and motivation. For example, time can seem to pass more quickly when we are engaged in activities we find enjoyable or when we are under stress. This research highlights the importance of considering the subjective experience of time in addition to its objective and physical aspects.

The current state of understanding the nature of time is a rapidly evolving and multi-disciplinary field, with researchers from a range of disciplines, including physics, philosophy, psychology, and cultural studies, contributing to our understanding of this complex and mysterious concept. The ongoing research and advancements in this field have the potential to deepen our understanding of the universe and lead to new insights into the nature of reality.

Chapter Twenty-Five:
Future Directions for Research and Exploration

Time is a complex and mysterious concept that has been studied for centuries by philosophers, scientists, and mathematicians. Despite our understanding of it, there are still many questions about the nature of time that remain unanswered. In this section, we will explore some of the future directions for research and exploration of time.

Theories of quantum gravity: Time and space are closely related concepts, and a full understanding of time requires a comprehensive theory of quantum gravity. This will likely involve merging quantum mechanics and general relativity, which currently appear to be incompatible. Research in this area is expected to lead to a deeper understanding of the nature of time and its relation to the fabric of the universe.

Time perception: Another area of research is the study of time perception, which is the way we experience time. It has been shown that our perception of time can be affected by a variety of factors, including attention, stress, and context. Further exploration of this area could lead to a better understanding of how the brain processes time and how it can be manipulated.

The Arrow of Time: The arrow of time is the direction in which time seems to flow, from the past to the future. This concept is still not well understood and is an area of active research. A deeper understanding of the arrow of time could lead to insights into the nature of time itself and the origin of the universe.

Time travel: Time travel is a popular topic in science fiction, but it is still purely speculative. However, there is ongoing research into the possibility of time travel and its implications for the nature of time and causality. This area is likely to continue to be an area of fascination and exploration.

The role of time in living organisms: Another area of research is the role of time in living organisms. This includes the study of circadian rhythms, the internal biological clocks that regulate the sleep-wake cycle and other physiological processes, as well as the study of aging and the processes that lead to the decline of physical and mental functions over time.

The study of time is a rich and interdisciplinary field, with many exciting areas for research and exploration. From the role of time in quantum mechanics to the role of time in decision making, there is much to be learned about the nature of time and its role in the universe.

Chapter Twenty-Six:
Evolution of Time

The evolution of time indeed represents a fascinating journey through human history, marked by both practical innovations and profound philosophical inquiries. Early civilizations relied on natural phenomena such as the movement of celestial bodies to measure time, laying the groundwork for our understanding of cyclical patterns and the concept of days, months, and years.

The development of mechanical clocks in the Middle Ages revolutionized timekeeping, allowing for more precise measurement and coordination of activities. This innovation not only facilitated advancements in science, navigation, and commerce but also fundamentally transformed social organization and labor practices.

The subsequent refinement of timekeeping technologies, including the invention of quartz and atomic clocks, has led to unprecedented levels of precision and accuracy in measuring time. These advancements have been instrumental in the establishment of standardized time zones and the synchronization of activities on a global scale, from international travel to telecommunications.

However, despite these remarkable technological achievements, the concept of time remains a subject of philosophical inquiry and scientific exploration. Questions about the nature of time, its relationship to space and causality, and the possibility of time travel continue to captivate the imagination of scientists, philosophers, and artists alike.

In physics, theories such as Einstein's theory of relativity have challenged our intuitive understanding of time, suggesting that it is not an absolute and unchanging entity but rather a dynamic and relative phenomenon influenced by gravity and velocity.

Moreover, advancements in fields such as quantum mechanics and cosmology have raised new questions about the nature of time at the smallest and largest scales of the universe, challenging our conventional notions of past, present, and future.

In the realm of philosophy, thinkers throughout history have grappled with the nature of time, exploring its role in shaping human experience, consciousness, and existence. From ancient philosophers such as Aristotle and Augustine to modern thinkers like Henri Bergson and Martin Heidegger, the concept of time has been a perennial source of fascination and debate.

The evolution of time is a testament to humanity's quest for understanding and mastery over the fundamental dimensions of existence. While advances in technology have revolutionized our ability to measure and coordinate time, the concept itself remains deeply intertwined with our understanding of the universe and our place within it, continuing to inspire curiosity and exploration across disciplines and cultures.

Chapter Twenty-Seven:
Definition of Evolution of Time

Time is a concept that has been studied and debated by philosophers, scientists, and mathematicians for centuries. Despite its widespread use and importance in our daily lives, there is still no universally agreed upon definition of time. However, one of the most influential definitions of time is that it is the progression of events in a linear and continuous manner.

This definition of time has evolved significantly over the course of human history. In the ancient world, time was often seen as cyclical, with events repeating themselves in an endless cycle of birth, death, and rebirth. This idea was reflected in the creation of calendars, which marked the passage of time based on the cycles of the moon and the seasons.

In the Middle Ages, time became more closely associated with the concept of eternity, with time seen as a linear progression towards an ultimate end point. This idea was closely tied to religious beliefs and the concept of a divine plan for the world.

With the advent of modern science, time took on a new meaning. In the 17th century, the philosopher and mathematician Isaac Newton defined time as a continuous and absolute quantity that flowed uniformly, regardless of any events that were occurring in the world. This idea was reflected in his laws of motion, which stated that the laws of nature were constant and unchanging, and that time was a necessary component of these laws.

However, this definition of time was challenged in the 20th century by the advent of Einstein's theory of relativity. Indeed, Albert Einstein's theory of relativity, formulated in the early 20th century, revolutionized our understanding of time and space. One of the key insights of Einstein's theory was the concept of time dilation, which states that time can pass at different rates for observers in different inertial reference frames, particularly when they are moving at significant fractions of the speed of light or are in strong gravitational fields.

Special relativity, published by Einstein in 1905, introduced the idea that time is relative and can be experienced differently by observers in motion relative to each other. According to this theory, as an object's velocity approaches the speed of light, time appears to slow down for that object relative to a stationary observer. This phenomenon, known as time dilation, has been experimentally confirmed and is a fundamental aspect of our understanding of the universe.

General relativity, developed by Einstein in 1915, extended these ideas to include the influence of gravity on the passage of time. In strong gravitational fields, such as those near massive objects like stars or black holes, time is further distorted, causing it to appear to pass more slowly for observers closer to the gravitational source. This effect, known as gravitational time dilation, has also been observed and confirmed through experiments and astronomical observations.

Einstein's theories of relativity have had profound implications for our understanding of the nature of time and space. They have provided a framework for reconciling the classical notions of space and time with the principles of electromagnetism and gravity, and have led to numerous technological applications, including the global positioning system (GPS), which relies on corrections for both special and general relativistic effects to provide accurate navigation.

In summary, Einstein's theory of relativity revolutionized our understanding of time by demonstrating that it is not an absolute and uniform quantity but rather a dynamic and relative phenomenon that can be influenced by factors such as motion and gravity. This insight has had far-reaching implications for both theoretical physics and everyday life, fundamentally reshaping our understanding of the universe and our place within it.

Today, our understanding of time continues to evolve, with ongoing research into the nature of time, the relationship between time and space, and the role of time in our lives and the universe. Despite the many definitions and theories that have been proposed over the years, one thing remains certain: time is a fundamental and essential part. One of the most fascinating aspects of the evolution of time is how it has been intertwined with our understanding of the physical universe. From the ancient belief in cyclical time, to the idea of a linear progression towards an end point, to the modern understanding of time as a relative quantity influenced by mass and energy, our view of time has been shaped by our understanding of the world around us.

Another interesting aspect of the evolution of time is how it has been linked to our understanding of human experience. Time is an integral part of our perception of the world, and affects everything from our memories and emotions, to our relationships and decisions. As our understanding of time has evolved, so too has our understanding of the role that time plays in our lives.

It is worth mentioning that the evolution of time is not just a matter of intellectual curiosity. It has practical implications for a wide range of fields, from physics and astronomy, to psychology and economics. For example, the concept of relative time has led to the development of GPS technology, which uses the relative positions of satellites to determine a user's location on the earth.

Besides its scientific and practical implications, the evolution of time has also had a profound impact on our culture and society. From the earliest calendars used to mark the passage of time and coordinate human activities, to the modern obsession with time management and productivity, our relationship with time has played a central role in shaping human civilization.

The study of time has also been an important part of philosophy, with philosophers exploring the nature of time, its relationship with the physical world, and its role in shaping our experience of the world. For example, the philosopher Immanuel Kant famously argued that time is a necessary condition of human experience, and that it is impossible to conceive of the world without a notion of time.

One of the most interesting questions raised by the evolution of time is what the future holds. With ongoing advancements in our understanding of the physical universe, and the role that time plays in it, it is possible that our definition of time will continue to evolve in the years to come.

The evolution of time is a complex and multifaceted subject that has had a profound impact on human thought, culture, and society. From its earliest beginnings as a cyclical concept linked to the cycles of the moon and seasons, to its current status as a relative quantity influenced by mass and energy, the evolution of time is a fascinating story that continues to unfold.

Chapter Twenty-Eight:
Importance of Understanding the Evolution of Time

Understanding the evolution of time is crucial for a variety of reasons. Time is a fundamental aspect of our lives, and its evolution has played a major role in shaping human civilizations, cultures, and technological advancements. In this article, we will explore the importance of understanding the evolution of time and its significance in our lives.

First, it is important to understand that time is not a constant. The concept of time has evolved over the centuries, and its definition has changed as human civilizations have developed. In the past, people relied on the movement of the sun, moon, and stars to measure time, while today we have developed highly sophisticated clocks and timepieces that allow us to measure time with incredible accuracy. This evolution of time measurement has had a profound impact on our ability to coordinate activities and manage resources.

Another reason why understanding the evolution of time is important is that it has helped shape our understanding of the universe. As our understanding of time has evolved, so has our understanding of the universe itself. For example, the discovery that the speed of light is constant and that time slows down as one approaches the speed of light was a major breakthrough in our understanding of the universe. This discovery has led to a better understanding of the nature of time and space, and has had a profound impact on fields such as physics, astronomy, and cosmology.

Furthermore, understanding the evolution of time is also important for historical purposes. The study of the evolution of time helps us understand how different cultures and civilizations have approached the concept of time and how it has shaped their beliefs and practices. For example, ancient civilizations like the Mayans and Egyptians had highly sophisticated systems for measuring time, which played a major role in their religious and cultural practices.

Understanding the evolution of time is also important for personal development. By understanding how the concept of time has evolved, we can gain a deeper appreciation for the present moment and how we can use our time in meaningful ways. For example, by recognizing the limitations of time and how it can shape our experiences, we can make better choices about how we spend our time and prioritize what is truly important in our lives.

Understanding the evolution of time is crucial for a variety of reasons. From shaping our understanding of the universe, to helping us better manage our time and resources, to providing insight into the beliefs and practices of different cultures, the evolution of time has played a major role in shaping our lives and the world around us.

Understanding the evolution of time also helps us understand the impact of technology on our perception of time. The invention of new technologies has often altered the way we measure and experience time. For example, the widespread use of computers, smartphones, and other digital devices has made it easier for us to stay connected and manage our time, but it has also created new challenges and pressures, such as the constant demands of being connected and the pressure to be productive 24/7.

Moreover, the evolution of time has also influenced our sense of identity and community. Time has been a critical factor in shaping our relationships, our social structures, and our cultural traditions. For example, the celebration of holidays and other special events helps bring people together and create a sense of community, while the observance of specific rituals and customs gives people a sense of belonging and helps reinforce their cultural identity.

Another aspect of the evolution of time that is worth mentioning is its impact on the environment. The way we measure and use time can have a significant impact on the natural world. For example, the development of modern agriculture has allowed us to produce more food in less time, but it has also led to the depletion of natural resources, such as soil and water, and the degradation of the environment.

It is worth noting that the evolution of time is not over. As new technologies continue to emerge, our understanding of time and how we measure it will continue to evolve. This means that it is essential for us to stay informed and adaptable, so that we can continue to make the most of the opportunities that time provides, while avoiding the potential pitfalls that come with new developments.

The evolution of time is an ongoing process that has had and will continue to have a profound impact on our lives, our understanding of the universe, and the world around us. By understanding the evolution of time, we can gain a deeper appreciation for the present moment, and make more informed choices about how we use our time and resources.

Besides the reasons mentioned above, understanding the evolution of time is also important for our personal and professional growth. Time management is a crucial skill that can help us achieve our goals and be more productive, both in our personal and professional lives. By understanding the historical and cultural context in which different time management practices have emerged, we can gain a deeper appreciation for the importance of this skill and how to use it effectively.

Moreover, the evolution of time has also had a major impact on our understanding of the economy. From the development of money and trade, to the invention of the clock and the rise of the industrial revolution, time has been a critical factor in shaping the economy and determining the distribution of wealth and resources. By understanding the evolution of time and its impact on the economy, we can gain a deeper appreciation for the factors that drive economic growth and development, and make more informed decisions about how to allocate our resources.

Another important aspect of the evolution of time is its impact on our understanding of psychology and human behavior. Time has been shown to have a profound impact on our moods, emotions, and behavior, and understanding its evolution can help us better understand how we experience and perceive time. For example, research has shown that the way we use and perceive time can influence our level of stress, our sense of well-being, and our overall happiness.

It is worth mentioning that the evolution of time has also had a major impact on the way we think and communicate. The invention of writing and the development of language have allowed us to preserve and transmit information and ideas across time and space.

Today, the internet and other digital technologies have made it easier than ever to access information and communicate with others, and this has transformed the way we think, learn, and interact with the world.

Understanding the evolution of time is essential for a variety of reasons, ranging from its impact on our personal and professional lives, to its influence on our understanding of the universe, the economy, psychology, and communication. By staying informed and aware of the ongoing evolution of time, we can gain a deeper appreciation for the present moment and make more informed choices about how we use our time and resources.

Chapter Twenty-Nine:
Time as a Relative Concept

Time is a concept that has fascinated humans for centuries. From ancient civilizations to modern physics, people have been trying to understand and measure time in various ways. Despite its significance, the concept of time remains one of the most elusive and relative phenomena in the universe.

At its most basic level, time is simply a measure of the duration between two events. We use clocks and calendars to keep track of time and to coordinate our daily activities. However, this understanding of time is limited, as it only applies in our everyday experiences. In the larger, cosmic context, time can behave very differently.

One of the most profound insights into the nature of time came from the theory of relativity, proposed by Albert Einstein. According to Einstein, time is not absolute and unchanging, but rather is relative to the observer. This means that time can appear to pass at different rates for different observers, depending on their relative motion and proximity to a source of gravity.

For example, if two people are moving at different speeds, each person will experience time differently. For the person moving at a slower speed, time will appear to pass more slowly, while for the person moving at a faster speed, time will appear to pass more quickly. This effect, known as time dilation, has been verified through numerous experiments and is considered one of the pillars of modern physics.

Besides time dilation, Einstein's theory of relativity also suggests that time can bend in the presence of strong gravitational fields. This means that time can flow more slowly near massive objects such as black holes, where the gravitational pull is so strong that it warps the fabric of space-time.

These effects, combined with our limited understanding of the universe and the nature of time itself, make it clear that time is a relative concept. It is dependent on the observer and the conditions under which they experience it. In this sense, time can be seen as a subjective experience, rather than an objective, unchanging reality.

While time may seem simple and straightforward in our daily lives, it is actually a complex and relative concept that remains one of the great mysteries of the universe. Whether we will ever fully understand the nature of time remains to be seen, but one thing is certain: the concept of time will continue to captivate and challenge us for many generations to come.

Another aspect of the relativity of time is related to the concept of simultaneity. According to Einstein, two events that are simultaneous for one observer may not be simultaneous for another observer who is moving relative to the first observer. This means that time is not only relative to the observer's motion, but also to their location in the universe.

This concept has important implications for our understanding of causality and the flow of events in the universe. For example, if two events appear to occur simultaneously for one observer, but not for another observer, it raises questions about which event was the cause and which was the effect.

The idea of time being relative also has implications for our understanding of the past and the future. According to

Einstein, the past, present, and future are not absolute and unchanging, but rather are relative to the observer. This means that what is past for one observer may be the future for another observer, and vice versa.

Furthermore, the relative nature of time means that it may not be possible to determine the absolute age of an object or event. For example, the age of a distant star can only be estimated relative to our position and motion in the universe. This makes it difficult to determine the absolute age of the universe itself, as our perception of time is limited by the relative motion of the observer.

The concept of time as a relative phenomenon is one of the most profound insights of modern physics. It challenges our understanding of time as a fixed and absolute entity, and instead suggests that it is dependent on the observer and the conditions under which they experience it. Understanding the relative nature of time is crucial for advancing our knowledge of the universe and the way in which events occur within it.

The relative nature of time also has practical applications in various fields, such as astronomy, navigation, and engineering. For example, GPS systems rely on the accurate measurement of time dilation in order to provide precise location information.

In the field of astronomy, the relative nature of time is used to explain the behavior of binary star systems, where two stars orbit a common center of mass. According to the theory of relativity, the stars in a binary system experience time differently, depending on their relative motion and proximity to each other. This has important implications for our understanding of the evolution of binary star systems, and the way in which they interact with their surroundings.

In engineering, the relative nature of time is taken into account in the design of high-speed systems, such as aircraft and spacecraft. When objects move at high speeds, they experience time differently than objects at rest, and this must be taken into account in order to ensure the safety and reliability of these systems.

The relative nature of time has important philosophical implications, as it challenges our traditional understanding of the passage of time and the nature of causality. Some philosophers have argued that the relative nature of time suggests that the past, present, and future are not absolute, but rather are dependent on the observer and the conditions under which they experience them.

The concept of time as a relative phenomenon is one of the most intriguing and far-reaching ideas in science. From its practical applications in various fields, to its philosophical implications, the relative nature of time continues to fascinate and challenge us in new and exciting ways. Whether we will ever fully understand the nature of time remains to be seen, but one thing is certain: the study of time will continue to be an important area of research for many years to come.

Chapter Thirty:
Explanation of the Evolution of Time

The evolution of time refers to the changes and developments in the way that humans have perceived and measured time over the course of history. Time is a fundamental aspect of human experience, and its evolution has been shaped by a combination of scientific, cultural, and technological advancements. From the earliest civilizations to the present day, people have developed increasingly sophisticated methods for measuring and dividing time, reflecting the growing importance of time in human society

In the past, time was often tied to the natural cycles of the sun, moon, and stars, and was used primarily for agricultural and religious purposes. For example, early civilizations such as the Egyptians, Greeks, and Romans divided the day into smaller units using sundials and water clocks, and used calendars to track the passing of the seasons and mark important events.

As human society became more complex, the need for more precise time measurement arose. This led to the development of more advanced timekeeping devices, such as mechanical clocks, and the standardization of time zones to accommodate the needs of transportation and communication.

In the modern era, time has become increasingly important in shaping our daily lives and our understanding of the world. Advances in science and technology have enabled us to understand time on a molecular and atomic level and to use it as a tool for understanding the natural world. For instance, the field of astronomy uses time to study the movements of celestial bodies and the evolution of the universe, while physics uses time to understand the behavior of matter and energy.

The evolution of time is an ongoing process that reflects the changing needs and understanding of humans throughout history. By studying the development of our concept of time, we gain a deeper understanding of the impact that time has on our daily lives and on the world around us.

Moreover, the evolution of time has also been shaped by cultural and social factors. Different cultures have had different perspectives on time and have used it to reflect their beliefs and values. For example, in some Eastern cultures, time is perceived as a more fluid and cyclical concept, whereas in Western cultures, time is often seen as a linear and sequential progression.

Time has played an important role in shaping our economic and political systems. For instance, the use of time-based work schedules and the establishment of standard business hours have become critical components of modern capitalism, while the creation of time zones has facilitated global communication and cooperation.

Moreover, our relationship with time has also had significant psychological and emotional effects. The modern fast-paced lifestyle has led to an increased emphasis on time management and efficiency and has created new challenges such as stress, burnout, and feelings of time poverty.

The evolution of time is an ongoing and multifaceted process that has had far-reaching impacts on the natural world, human society, and our individual lives. Understanding the evolution of time is essential for gaining a deeper appreciation of the role that time plays in shaping our world, and for developing a more nuanced perspective on the challenges and opportunities that time presents.

Additionally, understanding the evolution of time is also important for addressing contemporary issues related to time. For example, the advancement of technology and globalization has led to a more connected and fast-paced world, and has raised questions about the sustainability of our current relationship with time. The increasing demand for 24/7 accessibility and the blurring of boundaries between work and leisure has created new challenges and opportunities for individuals, organizations, and societies.

In this context, studying the evolution of time can help us to understand the historical and cultural roots of our current relationship with time, and to identify ways to address the challenges and seize the opportunities that this relationship presents. For example, by examining how different cultures have approached the relationship between time and work, we may be able to identify alternative models that promote greater balance and well-being.

Furthermore, understanding the evolution of time can also provide us with a deeper appreciation of the role that time has played in shaping human culture and history. From the earliest civilizations to the present day, time has been a critical factor in shaping our beliefs, values, and way of life. By studying the evolution of time, we gain a deeper understanding of how different cultures have approached the concept of time, and how this has influenced the development of human society.

Understanding the evolution of time is a crucial aspect of human knowledge and self-awareness. By studying the development of our concept of time and its impact on the natural world, human society, and our individual lives, we gain a deeper appreciation of the role that time plays in shaping our world, and a better understanding of the challenges and opportunities that time presents.

Chapter Thirty-One:
Pre-Modern Views of Time

Pre-modern views of time varied greatly among different cultures and civilizations. In many ancient societies, time was seen as cyclical, with events and seasons repeating in an eternal cycle. In contrast, other cultures saw time as linear, with a beginning, middle, and end to the universe.

In ancient Babylon, time was viewed as cyclical, with the concept of the "eternal return" being central to their religion and worldview. The Babylonians developed a sophisticated system of timekeeping, using a sex ageism (base 60) system to divide the day into smaller units, such as minutes and seconds. This system was later adopted by the ancient Sumerians and Akkadians, as well as the Mayans and other cultures in the Americas.

In ancient Greece, time was also seen as cyclical, but with a linear aspect added. The philosopher Heraclitus believed that time was a river that flowed continually and that everything changed constantly, while his contemporary Parmenides believed that change was an illusion and that reality was unchanging and eternal. The philosopher Aristotle believed in a linear view of time, with a beginning, middle, and end to the world and all events within it.

In ancient China, time was viewed as cyclical, with a belief in the repetition of historical events and the cyclical nature of the seasons and celestial movements. The ancient Chinese also developed a sophisticated system of timekeeping, using a six ageism system and dividing the day into smaller units, such as minutes and seconds.

In ancient India, time was seen as both cyclical and linear. The Hindu concept of "kalpa" saw time as an endless cycle of creation and destruction, while the Buddhist concept of "karma" saw time as linear, with each individual's actions determining their future experiences in a cause-and-effect chain.

In pre-Columbian Mesoamerican cultures, such as the Maya, time was viewed as cyclical and was closely tied to their religious beliefs and calendar systems. The Maya believed in a series of creation and destruction cycles, with each cycle lasting for a set amount of time and repeating endlessly. Their elaborate calendar system, which included the use of multiple calendars, was used to track the movements of the stars and planets, as well as to mark important religious and cultural events.

Pre-modern views of time were diverse and varied greatly among different cultures and civilizations. From the cyclical view of time in ancient Babylon, to the linear view in ancient Greece, to the dual view in ancient India, the ways in which people thought about time reflected the unique religious and cultural beliefs. Despite these differences, all of these cultures were able to develop sophisticated systems of timekeeping, reflecting the importance they placed on understanding and measuring the passage of time.

Chapter Thirty-Two:
Religious and Philosophical Views of Time

Time is one of the most fundamental and universal experiences of human existence. It is a concept that has been explored by many religious and philosophical traditions throughout history, each offering their own unique perspectives on the nature of time and its relationship to the world and human existence.

In the Western tradition, the concept of time has been heavily influenced by the philosophy of Aristotle, who argued that time is a measure of change and that it exists independently of any particular event. This view was later adopted by Christian theologians, who saw time as a linear progression that begins with the creation of the world and moves toward the end of time, the Day of Judgment. In this view, time is seen as a gift from God that gives humans the opportunity to repent and seek salvation.

In Eastern traditions, the concept of time has been approached in a more cyclical manner, with a focus on the idea that time is cyclical and repetitive, and that events and circumstances are continuously repeated in an endless cycle of birth, death, and rebirth. Hinduism and Buddhism, for example, see time as an illusion that exists only in the mind and that the true reality is eternal and unchanging.

In contrast to these religious views, many philosophers have seen time as a purely human construct, a tool that we use to understand the world around us. Immanuel Kant, for example, argued that time is not an objective property of the world, but rather a necessary form of human perception. Similarly, Henri Bergson saw time as a continuous flow that cannot be broken down into discrete moments, and that our experience of time is not a fixed and unchanging entity, but is instead shaped by our experiences and the way we engage with the world.

In the 20th century, physicists and philosophers have debated the nature of time in the context of the theory of relativity and quantum mechanics. Some have argued that time is a fundamental aspect of the universe and that it is woven into the fabric of space-time, while others have suggested that time is an emergent phenomenon that arises from the behavior of matter and energy in the universe.

The religious and philosophical views of time are diverse and varied, reflecting the different ways in which human beings have sought to understand and make sense of this elusive and mysterious concept. Whether seen as a linear progression, a cyclical repetition, a human construct, or a fundamental aspect of the universe, time remains a subject of ongoing exploration and debate, one that continues to challenge and inspire the human imagination.

Besides the Western, Eastern, and philosophical views of time discussed above, there are also many other religious and spiritual perspectives on time that are worth exploring.

In indigenous cultures, for example, time is often seen as cyclical and connected to the natural world, with the cycles of the moon, sun, and stars reflecting the cycles of life, death, and rebirth. In these traditions, time is not a linear progression, but rather a dance between the forces of nature and the spiritual world.

In certain strands of mysticism and spirituality, time is seen as an illusion that obscures the true nature of reality. In these traditions, time is viewed as a barrier to spiritual enlightenment and liberation, and it is only through meditation, contemplation, and other spiritual practices that one can transcend time and experience the timeless nature of reality.

In monotheistic traditions, such as Judaism, Christianity, and Islam, time is often seen as a gift from God, with a clear beginning and end, and with the purpose of allowing humans to repent and seek salvation. In these traditions, time is seen as both a test and an opportunity, and the way in which individuals use their time is seen as a reflection of their faith and commitment to God.

The religious and philosophical views of time are many and diverse, reflecting the different ways in which human beings have sought to understand and make sense of this fundamental aspect of our existence. Whether viewed as a linear progression, a cyclical repetition, a human construct, an illusion, or a gift from God, time remains a subject of ongoing exploration and debate, with each perspective offering its own unique insights into the nature of reality and our place in the world.

It's also worth mentioning that some religious and philosophical traditions have held that time itself is created by a divine being. In these views, time is seen as a product of the divine will and is therefore dependent on the deity's existence. For example, in Christianity, God is said to have created the world and all that exists within it, including time itself. This idea is reflected in the opening verses of the book of Genesis, which state that "In the beginning, God created the heavens and the earth."

In some Native American spiritual traditions, the universe is believed to have been created through a sacred act of singing, and time is seen as a result of this creation.

Similarly, in ancient Egyptian religion, the god Ra was said to have created the world through the power of his word, and time was seen as a product of this act of creation.

In many esoteric and mystical traditions, time is seen as a manifestation of divine consciousness and is therefore linked to the concept of the divine mind. In these views, the unfolding of time is seen as a reflection of the divine plan and is therefore intimately connected to the divine will.

Besides these religious and philosophical views of time, it is also worth noting that many scientists and philosophers have explored the nature of time in a more empirical and objective manner. In physics, for example, the concept of time is central to the study of space-time and the theory of relativity, and many scientists have sought to understand the nature of time and its relationship to the physical world. Similarly, in philosophy, many have explored the nature of time from a more abstract and theoretical perspective, using logical and analytical methods to shed light on this elusive and mysterious concept.

The religious and philosophical views of time are incredibly diverse, reflecting the different ways in which human beings have sought to understand this fundamental aspect of our existence. From religious and spiritual perspectives, to philosophical and scientific perspectives, the study of time continues to inspire and challenge us, as we seek to gain a deeper understanding of this mysterious and elusive concept.

Chapter Thirty-Three:
The Impact of These Views on the Understanding of Time

The concept of time has been a subject of philosophical inquiry for centuries, and as a result, there have been various views on the nature of time that have emerged over time. These views have had a profound impact on our understanding of time and have shaped the way in which we think about and experience the passage of time.

One of the most influential views of time is that of classical physics, which views time as an absolute and independent dimension. According to this view, time is a linear and irreversible progression that is independent of other physical phenomena and that can be precisely measured and recorded. This view of time was central to the development of classical mechanics and has been the foundation of our understanding of the physical world for centuries.

Another important view of time is that of relativity, which was developed by Albert Einstein. According to this view, time is relative to the observer and is dependent on their state of motion. This view challenged the classical view of time as an absolute and independent dimension, and it led to the development of the theory of relativity, which revolutionized our understanding of space and time.

A third view of time is that of quantum mechanics, which views time as a quantum variable that is subject to quantum fluctuations. According to this view, time is not a continuous and deterministic progression, but rather is subject to the indeterminacy and probabilistic nature of quantum mechanics. This view of time has challenged our classical understanding of time and has led to new and exciting developments in physics and quantum technology.

The various views of time have had a profound impact on our understanding of time and have shaped the way in which we think about and experience the passage of time. The classical view of time has provided us with a foundation for understanding the physical world, while the theory of relativity has challenged our assumptions about the nature of time and led to new discoveries about the relationship between space and time. The view of time in quantum mechanics has opened up new avenues for exploration and has led to the development of new technologies based on the principles of quantum mechanics.

The different views of time have played a crucial role in shaping our understanding of this fundamental aspect of our existence. As our understanding of time continues to evolve, it is likely that new perspectives will emerge that will further deepen and broaden our understanding of this elusive and fascinating concept.

The different views of time have also had a significant impact on other areas of human endeavor beyond the realm of physics. For example, the view of time as a continuous and irreversible progression has played a central role in shaping our understanding of history, while the theory of relativity has influenced our understanding of the nature of time and its relationship to space.

Moreover, the different views of time have also had an impact on our understanding of the human experience. The classical view of time as an absolute and independent dimension has led to the development of clocks and calendars, which have played a crucial role in organizing human societies and facilitating the coordination of human activity. On the other hand, the theory of relativity has challenged our assumptions about the objective nature of time and has led to new perspectives on the subjectivity of our experience of time.

The different views of time have also influenced our understanding of the nature of reality. The classical view of time as an absolute and independent dimension has led to the development of deterministic models of the physical world, while the theory of relativity has challenged this determinism and opened up new possibilities for understanding the indeterminacy and probabilistic nature of the universe.

The different views of time have had a profound impact on our understanding of time and have shaped the way in which we think about and experience the passage of time. From physics to history, from the human experience to the nature of reality, these views have influenced our understanding of the world in countless ways and have provided us with new perspectives and insights into the nature of time and existence.

The understanding of time is shaped by a number of different factors, including cultural, philosophical, and scientific views. These views can have a significant impact on the way individuals perceive and experience time, as well as the ways in which they organize and structure their lives.

For example, philosophical views of time can range from those that see time as an absolute, objective reality to those that view it as a subjective experience. Scientific views, on the other hand, may focus on the physical and mathematical nature of time, examining it as a dimension in which events occur in a linear and irreversible fashion.

Cultural views of time can also have a major impact on the understanding of time, with different cultures having different attitudes towards time and the way in which it is perceived and experienced. For example, some cultures may view time as a valuable commodity that should be used wisely and carefully, while others may view it as a more fluid and flexible concept that can be manipulated and shaped to suit one's needs.

The impact of these different views on the understanding of time is significant, as it affects how individuals perceive, experience, and use time in their daily lives. By exploring the different perspectives and attitudes towards time, individuals can gain a deeper understanding of the complex and multifaceted nature of this concept.

Chapter Thirty-Four:
Exploring the Theory of Serial Time: Insights from J.W. Dunne's "An Experiment in Time"

Time, the ever-elusive dimension that governs our lives, has been a subject of fascination and inquiry for centuries. From philosophers to physicists, humanity has grappled with the nature of time, seeking to understand its intricacies and mysteries. Among the myriad theories proposed to unravel its enigma, one that stands out is the theory of serial time, as expounded by J.W. Dunne in his seminal work "An Experiment in Time."

In this section, we delve into Dunne's theory of serial time, exploring its key concepts, implications, and significance in the realm of philosophy and beyond.

1. Introduction to Serial Time

J.W. Dunne, an aeronautical engineer by profession, embarked on a journey of exploration into the nature of time that transcended the boundaries of conventional scientific inquiry. In his book "An Experiment in Time," published in 1927, Dunne presents a theory that challenges our linear perception of time. He posits that time is not experienced as a continuous flow but rather as a series of interconnected moments, existing simultaneously in a higher dimension beyond our ordinary perception.

2. The Nature of Time

Central to Dunne's theory is the notion that time is not an absolute, unidirectional phenomenon but rather a multi-dimensional construct. He proposes that past, present, and future coexist in a timeless realm, accessible to consciousness through dreams and moments of heightened awareness. Dunne suggests that our experience of time is subjective, shaped by our perception and consciousness.

3. Dreams and Premonitions

Dunne draws extensively from his own experiences with dreams and premonitions to support his theory of serial time. He argues that dreams provide glimpses into alternate realities and future events, suggesting that our consciousness can transcend the constraints of linear time. According to Dunne, dreams serve as windows into the timeless realm where past, present, and future converge.

4. The Implications of Serial Time

Dunne's theory of serial time has profound implications for our understanding of reality and consciousness. It challenges the traditional view of time as a linear progression and opens up new possibilities for exploring the mysteries of existence. By suggesting that past, present, and future are interconnected and mutable, Dunne's theory invites us to reconsider our perception of causality and free will.

5. Criticisms and Reception

While Dunne's theory of serial time has garnered interest and intrigue, it has also faced criticism from skeptics and proponents of more conventional theories of time. Critics argue that Dunne's reliance on subjective experiences such as dreams undermines the scientific rigor of his theory. Moreover, the lack of empirical evidence to support his claims poses a challenge to the validity of his arguments.

Despite these criticisms, Dunne's work continues to inspire and provoke thought among philosophers, scientists, and enthusiasts alike. His exploration of time as a multi-dimensional phenomenon challenges us to expand our understanding of reality and embrace the mysteries that lie beyond the confines of our ordinary perception.

In conclusion, J.W. Dunne's theory of serial time offers a captivating glimpse into the nature of reality and consciousness. By challenging the linear conception of time and proposing a multi-dimensional framework, Dunne invites us to reconsider our place in the universe and the nature of existence itself. While his theory may remain speculative in nature, it serves as a catalyst for further exploration and inquiry into the enigmatic realm of time.

Chapter Thirty-Five:
Exploring the Theory of Three Dimensions of Time by P. Ouspensky

In the vast landscape of philosophical inquiry, few concepts challenge our fundamental understanding of reality as profoundly as the nature of time. Time, in its linear progression, has been a cornerstone of human experience, guiding our perception of past, present, and future. However, within the esoteric realms of metaphysics, there exist theories that delve deeper, questioning the conventional understanding of time as a unidimensional construct. Among these philosophical explorations stands the theory of the three dimensions of time, proposed by the Russian mystic and philosopher P. Ouspensky.

Peter Ouspensky, known for his work in the realms of mysticism, psychology, and philosophy, introduced the concept of the three dimensions of time in his seminal work "A New Model of the Universe." Ouspensky's theory challenges conventional notions of time by suggesting that time is not merely a linear progression but a multidimensional phenomenon encompassing past, present, and future in a dynamic interplay of existence.

The First Dimension of Time: Linear Time

Ouspensky begins his exploration by acknowledging the familiar notion of linear time, the one-dimensional flow that we perceive in our daily lives. This dimension of time is characterized by the sequential progression of events from past to present to future. It is the time we experience as we move through our lives, marked by the passage of moments, days, and years. Linear time provides us with a framework for understanding causality and the unfolding of events within the physical world.

The Second Dimension of Time: Vertical Time

Beyond the linear progression lies what Ouspensky refers to as vertical time, the second dimension of time. Unlike linear time, which flows in a single direction, vertical time encompasses the depth of experience, transcending the boundaries of past, present, and future. In this dimension, moments are not isolated points on a timeline but interconnected layers of consciousness, where past events exert influence on the present and future potentials ripple through the fabric of reality.

Vertical time introduces the concept of recurrence, suggesting that certain patterns and events recur across different points in time, creating echoes and resonances that shape our experience. Within this dimension, Ouspensky explores the idea of eternal recurrence, proposing that the universe undergoes cyclical patterns of creation and dissolution, with each cycle reflecting and building upon the previous ones.

The Third Dimension of Time: Eternal Now

At the pinnacle of Ouspensky's theory lies the third dimension of time, the eternal now. Here, past, present, and future converge into a timeless moment of pure existence. This dimension transcends the limitations of linear and vertical time, offering a glimpse into the ultimate reality where all possibilities exist simultaneously.

In the eternal now, Ouspensky suggests that time ceases to be a linear progression or a layered experience but becomes a state of being in which the individual transcends temporal boundaries and experiences the interconnectedness of all existence. It is a state of heightened awareness where the illusion of time dissolves, and the true nature of reality is revealed.

Implications and Applications

Ouspensky's theory of the three dimensions of time has profound implications for our understanding of consciousness, existence, and the nature of reality. By expanding our perception of time beyond its conventional boundaries, this theory invites us to reconsider our relationship with the past, present, and future, and to explore the interconnectedness of all moments.

Practically, this theory offers insights into various fields, including psychology, spirituality, and physics. In psychology, the concept of vertical time can inform therapeutic approaches by exploring the root causes of patterns and behaviors that extend beyond individual lifetimes. In spirituality, the idea of the eternal now opens pathways to transcendence and enlightenment, inviting practitioners to experience the unity of all creation. In physics, Ouspensky's theory resonates with concepts such as quantum entanglement and the block universe hypothesis, suggesting a deeper interplay between time and consciousness.

Conclusion

P. Ouspensky's theory of the three dimensions of time presents a provocative reimagining of the nature of temporal existence. By expanding beyond the confines of linear time, Ouspensky invites us to explore the depth and complexity of our temporal reality, from the sequential progression of events to the timeless realm of pure being. Whether as a philosophical inquiry or a practical framework for understanding consciousness, this theory challenges us to transcend our preconceived notions of time and embrace the vastness of temporal existence.

Chapter Thirty-Six:
Exploring Time: A Biblical Perspective

Time, an enigma that has fascinated humanity for centuries, is a concept deeply ingrained in the fabric of existence. From the rhythmic ticking of a clock to the grand cosmic cycles, time governs our lives in profound ways. But what does the Bible, one of the most revered religious texts, have to say about time and its nature?

In the Bible, time is not merely a chronological sequence of events but a divine construct with spiritual significance. It portrays time as both linear and cyclical, reflecting God's eternal nature and His sovereign control over all things.

The Linear and Cyclical Nature of Time

The Bible presents time as linear, unfolding in a sequence of past, present, and future. It begins with the creation narrative in Genesis, where God initiates time itself by declaring, "Let there be light" (Genesis 1:3). From this moment, time marches forward, carrying humanity through history towards a predetermined end.

Yet, the Bible also acknowledges the cyclical nature of time. Ecclesiastes 3:1-8 famously illustrates this duality, stating, "There is a time for everything, and a season for every activity under the heavens." This passage captures the rhythm of life, with its cycles of birth and death, planting and harvesting, weeping and laughing.

Time as a Tool of Divine Purpose

In biblical theology, time serves as a tool for God's divine purposes. He orchestrates events according to His perfect timing, fulfilling His promises and bringing about redemption. Galatians 4:4-5 highlights this, proclaiming, "But when the set time had fully come, God sent his Son, born of a woman, born under the law, to redeem those under the law."

Furthermore, the Bible teaches that God exists beyond the constraints of time. Psalm 90:4 poetically describes this concept, declaring, "A thousand years in your sight are like a day that has just gone by, or like a watch in the night." This verse emphasizes the eternal nature of God, who transcends the limitations of human timekeeping.

Living Intentionally in the Present

While acknowledging the past and anticipating the future, the Bible exhorts believers to live intentionally in the present moment. Jesus Himself emphasized the importance of seizing the present opportunity for spiritual growth and service. In Matthew 6:34, He instructs, "Therefore do not worry about tomorrow, for tomorrow will worry about itself. Each day has enough trouble of its own."

This emphasis on present living encourages mindfulness and gratitude, recognizing each moment as a gift from God. It fosters a deeper appreciation for the fleeting nature of time and the need to make the most of every opportunity for righteousness and love.

The Bible offers profound insights into the nature of time, portraying it as both linear and cyclical, a tool of divine purpose, and a call to intentional living. By understanding time through a biblical lens, we gain perspective on our place in God's eternal plan and are inspired to make the most of every moment entrusted to us.

As we reflect on the verses below, may we be reminded of the timelessness of God's love and the urgency of living faithfully in the present:

Genesis 1:1 - "In the beginning God created the heavens and the earth."

Ecclesiastes 3:1 - "There is a time for everything, and a season for every activity under the heavens."

Galatians 4:4-5 - "But when the set time had fully come, God sent his Son, born of a woman, born under the law, to redeem those under the law."

Psalm 90:4 - "A thousand years in your sight are like a day that has just gone by, or like a watch in the night."

Matthew 6:34 - "Therefore do not worry about tomorrow, for tomorrow will worry about itself. Each day has enough trouble of its own."

2 Peter 3:8 - "But do not forget this one thing, dear friends: With the Lord a day is like a thousand years, and a thousand years are like a day."

Ephesians 5:16 - "making the most of every opportunity, because the days are evil."

James 4:14 - "Why, you do not even know what will happen tomorrow. What is your life? You are a mist that appears for a little while and then vanishes."

Psalm 39:4 - "Show me, Lord, my life's end and the number of my days; let me know how fleeting my life is."

Colossians 4:5 - "Be wise in the way you act toward outsiders; make the most of every opportunity."

These verses further underscore the transient nature of time and the importance of using it wisely for spiritual growth and service to others. These verses serve as poignant reminders of God's sovereignty over time and His call to live purposefully in His eternal presence. May we heed this call and journey through time with faith, hope, and love as our guiding lights.

Chapter Thirty-Seven:
The Theory of Eternal Return: Exploring Time's Infinite Loop

Time, the enigmatic force that governs the universe, has been a subject of fascination and speculation for millennia. Among the many theories attempting to grasp its essence, one particularly intriguing concept is that of eternal return or eternal recurrence. This theory suggests that time is not a linear progression but rather a cyclical phenomenon, wherein events repeat infinitely. In this section, we delve into the depths of the theory of eternal return, exploring its origins, its philosophical implications, and its relationship with the nature of time itself.

Origins of the Theory

The roots of the theory of eternal return can be traced back to ancient civilizations, notably in the works of Eastern philosophies such as Hinduism and Buddhism, where the concept of reincarnation embodies a similar cyclical view of existence. However, it was the German philosopher Friedrich Nietzsche who popularized the notion of eternal return in Western thought during the 19th century. In his work "Thus Spoke Zarathustra," Nietzsche presents the idea of the eternal recurrence as a thought experiment, challenging individuals to confront the possibility that their lives, with all their triumphs and tribulations, might repeat infinitely.

Philosophical Implications

At its core, the theory of eternal return raises profound existential questions about the nature of existence and the human condition. If time is indeed cyclical, and events recur infinitely, what does this mean for individual identity and free will? Are our lives predetermined, or do we have the power to break free from the cycle? These questions have captivated philosophers, theologians, and thinkers throughout history, fueling debates on determinism versus free will and the meaning of life itself.

For Nietzsche, the concept of eternal return served as a test of one's affirmation of life. Embracing the idea that one's actions would be repeated for eternity, Nietzsche argued, could lead to a profound sense of responsibility and empowerment. Rather than being weighed down by the burden of existence, individuals could find liberation in the realization that every moment is precious and worth living to its fullest.

Relationship with the Nature of Time

The theory of eternal return challenges conventional notions of time as a linear progression from past to present to future. Instead, it suggests that time is a closed loop, with no beginning or end. This view resonates with certain interpretations of modern physics, particularly in the realm of cosmology and quantum mechanics.

In cosmology, the concept of a cyclic universe proposes that the universe undergoes endless cycles of expansion and contraction, with each cycle resembling the one before it. While this idea remains speculative and subject to ongoing research, it highlights the possibility of time's cyclical nature on a cosmic scale.

In quantum mechanics, the notion of time's arrow becomes blurred, as fundamental particles exhibit behaviors that defy traditional notions of cause and effect. Concepts such as quantum superposition and entanglement suggest that events may not unfold in a linear fashion but rather exist simultaneously across multiple timelines.

The theory of eternal return invites us to reconsider our perception of time and existence. Whether viewed through the lens of philosophy, physics, or spirituality, the idea of events repeating infinitely challenges us to confront the mysteries of the universe and our place within it. While the concept may remain speculative and elusive, its enduring appeal lies in its ability to provoke thought and spark imagination. In embracing the possibility of eternal recurrence, we are confronted with the profound realization that time, like life itself, may be far more complex and mysterious than we can ever fully comprehend.

Chapter Thirty-Eight:
Unveiling Kozyrev's Properties of Time: A Journey into the Nature of Temporality

In the realm of theoretical physics, the concept of time remains one of the most enigmatic and captivating subjects. Among the various theorists who have ventured into this intricate domain, Nikolai Alexandrovich Kozyrev stands out for his profound insights into the nature of time. Kozyrev's properties of time delve into the essence of temporality, offering a unique perspective that challenges conventional notions. This section explores Kozyrev's theories, unraveling the complexities of time and its implications for our understanding of the universe.

Time, the elusive force that governs our existence, has intrigued philosophers, scientists, and thinkers for centuries. Nikolai Kozyrev, a Soviet astrophysicist and cosmologist, made significant contributions to our understanding of time through his groundbreaking research. Kozyrev's properties of time propose a novel framework that transcends traditional interpretations, shedding light on the intricate dynamics of temporal phenomena. This section delves into Kozyrev's theories, examining their implications for cosmology, quantum mechanics, and our perception of reality.

Kozyrev's Properties of Time:

Kozyrev's exploration of time revolves around several key properties, each offering profound insights into the nature of temporality:

Active Medium: Kozyrev posited that time is not a passive backdrop but rather an active medium with its own dynamics and characteristics. According to his theory, time possesses energy and exerts influence on physical processes, challenging the classical view of time as a mere parameter.

Temporal Density: Kozyrev proposed the concept of temporal density, suggesting that time is not uniformly distributed but varies in density across different regions of space. This temporal gradient influences the flow of time, affecting the rate at which events unfold.

Temporal Torsion: One of Kozyrev's most intriguing ideas is the notion of temporal torsion, which describes the twisting or spiraling motion of time. This torsional aspect of time can manifest as anomalous effects, such as temporal anomalies or deviations from classical predictions.

Nonlocality: Kozyrev's properties of time also imply a form of nonlocality, where temporal interactions transcend spatial boundaries. This nonlocal aspect of time challenges our conventional understanding of causality and opens up new possibilities for the interconnectedness of events.

Consciousness and Time:

Kozyrev speculated on the relationship between consciousness and time, suggesting that human perception plays a fundamental role in shaping temporal experiences. According to his theory, consciousness may interact with the temporal medium, influencing subjective experiences of time.

Implications for Cosmology and Quantum Mechanics: Kozyrev's properties of time have profound implications for both cosmology and quantum mechanics:

Cosmological Evolution: Kozyrev's insights into the dynamic nature of time offer a new perspective on the evolution of the universe. By considering time as an active medium, cosmologists can explore how temporal dynamics shape the formation and evolution of cosmic structures.

Quantum Entanglement: The concept of temporal nonlocality has parallels with the phenomenon of quantum entanglement, where particles exhibit correlations that transcend spatial distances. Kozyrev's theories suggest that time itself may be entangled, leading to novel interpretations of quantum phenomena.

Time Travel: While Kozyrev did not explicitly address time travel, his theories provide a framework for exploring the possibility of temporal manipulation. By understanding the active properties of time, physicists may one day unlock the secrets of time travel, albeit within the confines of theoretical speculation.

Challenges and Future Directions:

Despite its profound implications, Kozyrev's theory of time faces several challenges and unanswered questions:

Experimental Verification: Validating Kozyrev's properties of time experimentally remains a formidable task, given the subtle nature of temporal phenomena. Researchers continue to explore novel experimental techniques to probe the dynamics of time and verify theoretical predictions.

Integration with Quantum Gravity: Integrating Kozyrev's theory of time with quantum gravity remains an open question in theoretical physics. Bridging the gap between quantum mechanics and general relativity is essential for developing a comprehensive understanding of the nature of time.

Philosophical Implications: Kozyrev's theory raises profound philosophical questions about the nature of reality, causality, and the role of consciousness. Exploring these philosophical implications requires interdisciplinary collaboration and dialogue across various fields of inquiry.

Conclusion: Nikolai Kozyrev's properties of time offer a compelling framework for understanding the dynamic nature of temporality. By challenging conventional notions of time as a passive parameter, Kozyrev invites us to explore the active properties of time and their profound implications for our understanding of the universe. As researchers continue to unravel the mysteries of time, Kozyrev's theories serve as a guiding light, illuminating the path towards a deeper comprehension of the nature of temporality and our place within the fabric of spacetime.

Chapter Thirty Nine:
Exploring the Mysteries: The Nature of Time and the Theory of the Multiverse

Time, the elusive fabric that weaves through the tapestry of existence, has captivated human curiosity for millennia. From ancient philosophers to modern physicists, the quest to comprehend its essence has led to profound insights and provocative theories. Among these theories stands the concept of the multiverse, a mind-bending hypothesis that challenges our very perception of reality. In this exploration, we delve into the nature of time and the tantalizing theory of the multiverse, seeking to unravel the mysteries that lie at the intersection of these profound concepts.

The Enigma of Time:

Time, as we perceive it, flows inexorably from past to present to future, a relentless march that shapes our experiences and perceptions. Yet, beneath this apparent simplicity lies a complexity that defies easy understanding. For centuries, philosophers and scientists have grappled with the nature of time, probing its mysteries and uncovering layers of intricacy.

One of the most fundamental questions surrounding time is whether it is an objective feature of the universe or merely a subjective illusion. In classical physics, time is treated as an absolute and universal quantity, flowing uniformly for all observers. However, the advent of Einstein's theory of relativity shattered this notion, revealing that time is not an immutable entity but rather a dynamic and malleable dimension.

According to the theory of relativity, time is intimately linked with space in a four-dimensional continuum known as spacetime. Gravity warps this spacetime fabric, causing time to dilate and stretch in the presence of massive objects. This phenomenon, known as time dilation, has been experimentally confirmed and lies at the heart of modern cosmology.

Yet, despite these insights, the true nature of time remains elusive. Quantum mechanics further complicates the picture, suggesting that time may not be as linear and deterministic as we once believed. The concept of "quantum time," where events unfold probabilistically and backwards causation is possible, challenges our conventional understanding of cause and effect.

The Multiverse:

Against this backdrop of temporal mystery arises the theory of the multiverse, a concept that pushes the boundaries of our imagination to the limits. The multiverse proposes that our universe is just one of countless others, each existing in parallel and governed by its own unique laws and constants.

The origins of the multiverse idea can be traced back to quantum mechanics and cosmology. In the realm of quantum mechanics, the principle of superposition allows particles to exist in multiple states simultaneously until observed, giving rise to the notion of parallel realities. In cosmology, the theory of cosmic inflation suggests that the universe underwent a rapid expansion in its early stages, generating an infinite expanse of space-time with regions beyond our observable universe.

Within this vast multiverse landscape, each universe may possess different physical properties, constants, and even fundamental laws of nature. Some universes may resemble our own, while others may be radically different, harboring exotic forms of matter, alternate dimensions, or even different forms of life.

The multiverse hypothesis offers a compelling explanation for the fine-tuning of our universe, the seemingly improbable set of conditions necessary for the emergence of life. In a multiverse scenario, the existence of countless universes with varied properties increases the likelihood of at least one possessing the conditions conducive to life as we know it.

However, the multiverse remains a highly speculative concept, lacking empirical evidence to definitively confirm its existence. Critics argue that invoking an infinite number of universes to explain our own may be tantamount to invoking a deus ex machina, a convenient but unsubstantiated solution to cosmological puzzles.

Concluding Thoughts:

The nature of time and the theory of the multiverse stand as two of the most intriguing and enigmatic concepts in modern science. While our understanding of time has deepened through the insights of relativity and quantum mechanics, many mysteries remain unresolved. Similarly, the multiverse offers a tantalizing glimpse into the possibility of parallel realities, yet its existence remains a matter of speculation.

As we continue to probe the depths of reality, these questions will undoubtedly persist, driving us to explore new frontiers of knowledge and expand the boundaries of human understanding. Whether time is an illusion, a fundamental aspect of reality, or something altogether beyond our comprehension, and whether the multiverse is a cosmic reality or a product of theoretical speculation, one thing remains certain: the quest for answers will continue to fuel our curiosity and drive the relentless pursuit of truth.

Chapter Forty:
Exploring the Prospects of Time Travel: A Journey into the Unknown

Time travel has long been a fascination for humanity, capturing the imagination of scientists, writers, and dreamers alike. From H.G. Wells' classic novel "The Time Machine" to modern blockbuster films like "Back to the Future," the concept of traversing through time has intrigued and perplexed generations. But beyond its portrayal in popular culture, what are the real prospects of time travel? Is it merely a fanciful idea confined to the realms of science fiction, or could it one day become a reality?

Theoretical Framework

In the realm of theoretical physics, the concept of time travel is not outright dismissed. Albert Einstein's theory of relativity laid the groundwork for understanding the interplay between space and time, suggesting that time is not a fixed, immutable dimension but rather a dynamic entity that can be influenced by gravity and velocity.

One of the most prominent theories that allows for the possibility of time travel is the concept of wormholes. These hypothetical tunnels through spacetime could potentially connect distant points in space and time, allowing for a shortcut between different eras. While the existence of wormholes remains purely speculative, their theoretical possibility has fueled much speculation and scientific inquiry.

Challenges and Paradoxes

However, the prospect of time travel is not without its challenges and paradoxes. The most famous of these is the grandfather paradox, which posits that if one were to travel back in time and prevent one's own grandfather from meeting one's grandmother, thereby preventing one's own existence, a logical contradiction arises. Such paradoxes have led some physicists to argue that time travel may be fundamentally impossible, as it would violate the principles of causality and create logical inconsistencies.

Additionally, the energy requirements for traversing through time are thought to be immense, far beyond anything currently achievable with our existing technology. Theoretical models suggest that the energy needed to create and stabilize a traversable wormhole would be equivalent to the mass-energy of entire planets or even stars, presenting a formidable barrier to practical implementation.

Ethical and Philosophical Implications

Beyond the scientific and technical challenges, time travel raises profound ethical and philosophical questions. The ability to alter the past could have far-reaching consequences, potentially leading to unintended and catastrophic outcomes. Moreover, the very act of traveling through time raises questions about personal identity and the nature of free will. If one were to change events in the past, would the future unfold differently, or are certain events predestined to occur regardless of our interventions?

Exploring Alternative Conceptions

While the conventional notion of time travel involves physically journeying through time, some physicists have proposed alternative conceptions that may be more feasible. For instance, the concept of "time dilation" from Einstein's theory of relativity suggests that time can pass at different rates for observers in different frames of reference. Thus, a spaceship traveling at near-light speed would experience time differently than an observer on Earth, effectively allowing for a form of time travel into the future.

Similarly, quantum mechanics offers intriguing possibilities for temporal manipulation through phenomena such as quantum entanglement and superposition. While still in the realm of speculation, these quantum effects hint at the potential for novel approaches to understanding and harnessing the mysteries of time.

The prospects of time travel remain an enigma, tantalizingly close yet maddeningly elusive. While theoretical frameworks within physics offer glimpses of possibility, the practical realization of time travel poses daunting challenges and raises profound questions about the nature of reality itself. Whether humanity will one day unlock the secrets of temporal manipulation or whether time travel will forever remain the stuff of science fiction, only time will tell. In the meantime, the quest to understand the mysteries of time continues to inspire awe and wonder, driving scientific inquiry and sparking the imagination of generations to come.

Chapter Forty-One:
Key Points of Time

Time is a fundamental concept that has been central to human civilization for thousands of years. It is a measure of the progression of events and is used to structure our lives and understand the world around us. Here are the key points of time:

Definition of Time: Time is a continuous sequence of events that can be measured and is used to describe the progression of events.

Time as a dimension: Time is often considered as the fourth dimension, alongside the three dimensions of space (length, width, and height). This concept of time as a dimension helps us understand how events unfold in a linear progression.

Time units: Time can be measured in a variety of units, including seconds, minutes, hours, days, weeks, months, and years.

Timekeeping: The measurement of time has been central to human civilization for thousands of years, with early civilizations using the sun, moon, and stars to track the progression of time. Today, time is kept using atomic clocks, which are based on the vibrations of atoms and provide a precise and accurate measurement of time.

Time and motion: Time and motion are closely related concepts, with time being used to measure the progression of motion. The laws of motion, as described by Sir Isaac Newton, are based on the concept of time and describe how objects move and change over time.

Time and relativity: The theory of relativity, developed by Albert Einstein, explains how time can be affected by the presence of massive objects and the speed of an object relative to other objects. According to the theory of relativity, time passes more slowly in a stronger gravitational field and at higher speeds.

Time and perception: Our perception of time is subjective and can be affected by a variety of factors, including stress, attention, and emotion. This subjective nature of time is why time can seem to move more quickly or more slowly depending on the situation.

Time is a complex and multi-faceted concept that has been central to human civilization for thousands of years. It is used to structure our lives, understand the progression of events, and help us make sense of the world around us.

Chapter Forty-Two:
Recap of Key Points

In today's fast-paced world, it is crucial to stay up-to-date with the latest information and developments in various fields. However, with the constant influx of new information, it can be challenging to keep track of everything. This is where recapping key points can be extremely helpful.

Recapping key points involves summarizing essential information into concise and straightforward bullet points or short paragraphs. It helps to organize information and retain the most important details for future reference. Here are some of the benefits of recapping key points:

Improved Understanding: Recapping key points allows you to grasp the information in a more organized and systematic manner. By breaking down complex information into manageable pieces, you can better understand the material and retain it in your memory.

Increased Retention: Recapping key points can help you retain information for longer periods of time. When you summarize information into bite-sized pieces, it is easier to remember and recall when needed.

Time-Saving: Recapping key points saves time as it eliminates the need to go through lengthy articles, videos or presentations. You can quickly scan the recap to get a good idea of the key takeaways without having to invest a lot of time.

Better Preparation: Recapping key points can help you prepare for exams, meetings, and other events where you need to recall information quickly. It makes it easier to recall important details and reduces stress by providing a quick reference point.

Enhanced Communication: Recapping key points can also help improve communication. By summarizing information into concise and easy-to-understand bullet points, it becomes easier to share the information with others.

Recapping key points is a valuable tool for organizing, retaining and communicating information. Whether you are studying for an exam, preparing for a meeting, or simply trying to keep track of new developments, recapping key points can be a great way to stay on top of things.

When recapping key points, you are forced to analyze the information and determine what is truly important and relevant. This requires you to think critically about the information and make decisions about what to include and what to exclude. By practicing this type of analysis and decision-making, you can improve your critical thinking skills over time.

Recapping key points is also a great way to review information before an exam or important meeting. By summarizing the information, you can quickly identify any areas where you may need to focus your study or preparation. This can be especially helpful if you are dealing with a large amount of information, as it can be overwhelming to try to remember everything.

Recapping key points can be beneficial for personal development and self-reflection. By summarizing your experiences, thoughts, and insights, you can gain a better understanding of yourself and your growth over time. This can be especially useful for tracking your progress in areas such as personal growth, career development, and relationships.

Recapping key points can also help to foster collaboration and teamwork. When working in a group, it is important to be on the same page and understand each other's perspectives. By sharing a recap of key points, team members can ensure that everyone is on the same page and has a clear understanding of the project's goals and objectives.

Recapping key points is a useful and versatile tool for a variety of purposes. Whether you are studying for an exam, preparing for a meeting, or simply looking to organize your thoughts, recapping key points can help you retain information, improve your critical thinking skills, and foster collaboration. By taking the time to summarize and review information, you can make the most of your time and resources.

Chapter Forty-Three:
The Temporal Perspective from a Physical Standpoint

The physical approach to time is a view that considers time as a fundamental aspect of the physical universe. This view is rooted in the principles of physics and is based on the idea that time is a dimension in which events occur in a linear progression.

According to this approach, time can be measured by devices such as clocks and timers, and its progression can be affected by physical phenomena such as the relative velocity of an observer and the presence of a strong gravitational field. This view is supported by theories such as Einstein's theory of relativity, which describes how time behaves in different physical contexts.

One of the key insights of the physical approach to time is that time is relative and its rate of progression can vary depending on the observer's relative velocity and proximity to a gravitational field. This has important implications for our understanding of the physical universe and the nature of reality.

Another important aspect of the physical approach to time is that it is considered to be irreversible. This means that events occur in a linear progression, and it is not possible to return to an earlier moment in time. This feature of time is thought to play a crucial role in the evolution of the universe and in the development of complex physical systems.

The physical perspective on time regards it as a foundational element of the universe, akin to a dimension where events unfold in a linear sequence. Grounded in the principles of physics, this viewpoint finds support in theories like Einstein's theory of relativity, offering valuable insights into the essence of time and its impact on our comprehension of the physical realm

.

The physical approach to time also has important implications for our understanding of the nature of time. By considering time as a dimension, it allows us to better understand how events are related to each other and how they unfold over time. This perspective also provides a framework for understanding the behavior of physical systems, from the smallest subatomic particles to the largest structures in the universe.

Furthermore, the physical approach to time provides a way to study the evolution of the universe and the development of complex physical systems. By considering how time affects the progression of events, we can gain insight into the underlying physical processes that shape the universe. This perspective also provides a basis for exploring the interplay between time and other physical quantities, such as energy, momentum, and entropy.

The physical approach to time has important implications for our understanding of time travel and the possibility of time travel in the future. While time travel remains purely speculative, the study of time from a physical perspective provides a valuable foundation for exploring this intriguing possibility.

The physical approach to time provides a valuable perspective on the nature of time and its role in shaping our understanding of the physical world. By considering time as a dimension and exploring its behavior in different physical contexts, we can gain a deeper understanding of the nature of time and its relationship to the physical universe.

Another important aspect of the physical approach to time is that it provides a framework for understanding the relationship between time and space. In many physical theories, time and space are seen as interrelated aspects of a single four-dimensional space-time. This view provides a way to understand how physical objects and events are related to each other, and how they are affected by the curvature of space-time caused by the presence of matter and energy.

The physical approach to time also has important implications for our understanding of the nature of cause and effect. By considering time as a dimension, we can study the sequence of events that lead up to a particular outcome. This allows us to better understand the underlying physical processes that give rise to specific phenomena, and provides a framework for making predictions about the future.

The physical approach to time is closely tied to the study of entropy and the second law of thermodynamics. According to this law, the entropy of a closed system will always increase over time. This has important implications for our understanding of the evolution of the universe and the ultimate fate of the physical world.

The physical approach to time provides a way to explore the relationship between time and consciousness. Some researchers have explored the possibility that the subjective experience of time is tied to physical processes in the brain, and that the perception of time is influenced by a range of factors, including attention, memory, and sensory input.

The physical approach to time provides a valuable perspective on the nature of time and its relationship to the physical universe. By considering time as a dimension and exploring its behavior in different physical contexts, we can gain a deeper understanding of the nature of time and its role in shaping our understanding of the world around us.

References:

Le Poidevin, R., & MacBeath, M. (Eds.). (1993). The Philosophy of Time. Oxford University Press.

"About Time: Einstein's Unfinished Revolution" by Paul Davies (1996)

Davies, P. (1996). About Time: Einstein's Unfinished Revolution. Simon & Schuster.

"Time: A User's Guide" by Stefan Klein (2013)

Klein, S. (2013). Time: A User's Guide. Scribe Publications.

"Time's Arrow: The Origins of Thermodynamic Behavior" by Martin H. Krieger (1996)

Krieger, M. H. (1996). Time's Arrow: The Origins of Thermodynamic Behavior. Harvard University Press.

"Time and Free Will: An Essay on the Immediate Data of Consciousness" by Henri Bergson (1910)

Bergson, H. (1910). Time and Free Will: An Essay on the Immediate Data of Consciousness. Dover Publications.

"Introducing Time: A Graphic Guide" by Craig Callender and Ralph Edney (2000)

Callender, C., & Edney, R. (2000). Introducing Time: A Graphic Guide. Icon Books.

"Now and Then: From Coney Island to Here" by Joseph Heller (1998)

Heller, J. (1998). Now and Then: From Coney Island to Here. Simon & Schuster.

"The Labyrinth of Time: Introducing the Universe" by Michael Lockwood (2005)

Lockwood, M. (2005). The Labyrinth of Time: Introducing the Universe. Oxford University Press.

"Time's Arrow, Time's Cycle: Myth and Metaphor in the Discovery of Geological Time" by Stephen Jay Gould (1987)

Gould, S. J. (1987). Time's Arrow, Time's Cycle: Myth and Metaphor in the Discovery of Geological Time. Harvard University Press.

"The Order of Time Revisited" by Julian Barbour (2019)

Barbour, J. (2019). The Order of Time Revisited. Oxford University Press.

"Time and the Technosphere: The Law of Time in Human Affairs" by José Argüelles (2002)

Argüelles, J. (2002). Time and the Technosphere: The Law of Time in Human Affairs. Bear & Company.

"The Psychology of Time Perception" edited by Simon Grondin (2008)

Grondin, S. (Ed.). (2008). The Psychology of Time Perception. Emerald Group Publishing Limited.

"The Nature of Time" edited by Raymond Flood, Michael Lockwood, and Paul C. P. Humphreys (1986)

Flood, R., Lockwood, M., & Humphreys, P. C. P. (Eds.). (1986). The Nature of Time. Basil Blackwell.

"The Book of Time: The Secrets of Time, How It Works and How We Measure It" by Adam Hart-Davis (2004)

Hart-Davis, A. (2004). The Book of Time: The Secrets of Time, How It Works and How We Measure It. Firefly Books.

"Time's Arrows Today: Recent Physical and Philosophical Work on the Direction of Time" edited by Steven F. Savitt (1995)

Savitt, S. F. (Ed.). (1995). Time's Arrows Today: Recent Physical and Philosophical Work on the Direction of Time. Cambridge University Press.

"The Oxford Handbook of Philosophy of Time" edited by Craig Callender (2011)

Callender, C. (Ed.). (2011). The Oxford Handbook of Philosophy of Time. Oxford University Press.

"The Arrow of Time: A Voyage Through Science to Solve Time's Greatest Mystery" by Peter Coveney and Roger Highfield (1991)

Coveney, P., & Highfield, R. (1991). The Arrow of Time: A Voyage Through Science to Solve Time's Greatest Mystery. Fawcett Columbine.

"Time and the Space-Traveller" by J.B.S. Haldane (1928)

Haldane, J. B. S. (1928). Time and the Space-Traveller. Harper & Brothers.

"The Dance of Time: The Origins of the Calendar" by Michael Judge (1990)

Judge, M. (1990). The Dance of Time: The Origins of the Calendar. Four Walls Eight Windows.

"Time and Space" by Barry Dainton (2001)

Dainton, B. (2001). Time and Space. McGill-Queen's University Press.

"Time: From Earth Rotation to Atomic Physics" by Julian Schwinger (1997)

Schwinger, J. (1997). Time: From Earth Rotation to Atomic Physics. Dover Publications.

"The Time of Our Lives: The Ethics of Common Sense" by Tom Nagel (2012)

Nagel, T. (2012). The Time of Our Lives: The Ethics of Common Sense. Oxford University Press.

"Time and the Other: How Anthropology Makes Its Object" by Johannes Fabian (2002)

Fabian, J. (2002). Time and the Other: How Anthropology Makes Its Object. Columbia University Press.

"The Power of Time Perception: Control the Speed of Time to Make Every Second Count" by Jean Paul Zogby (2017)

Zogby, J. P. (2017). The Power of Time Perception: Control the Speed of Time to Make Every Second Count. Archangel Ink.

"The Lure of the Edge: Scientific Passions, Religious Beliefs, and the Pursuit of UFOs" by Brenda Denzler (2001)

Denzler, B. (2001). The Lure of the Edge: Scientific Passions, Religious Beliefs, and the Pursuit of UFOs. University of California Press.

"The Metaphysics of Time" edited by Michael J. Loux and Dean W. Zimmerman (2009)

Loux, M. J., & Zimmerman, D. W. (Eds.). (2009). The Metaphysics of Time. Oxford University Press.

"Theories of Time: From Parmenides to Einstein" by Michael Tooley (1999)

Tooley, M. (1999). Theories of Time: From Parmenides to Einstein. Routledge.

"The End of Time: The Next Revolution in Our Understanding of the Universe" by Julian Barbour (1999)

Barbour, J. (1999). The End of Time: The Next Revolution in Our Understanding of the Universe. Weidenfeld & Nicolson.

"Time: A Philosophical Introduction" by Robin Le Poidevin (2010)

Le Poidevin, R. (2010). Time: A Philosophical Introduction. Bloomsbury Academic.

"The Book of Time: Everything You Need to Know About the Biggest Idea in the Universe" by Adam Hart-Davis (2002)

Hart-Davis, A. (2002). The Book of Time: Everything You Need to Know About the Biggest Idea in the Universe. Metro Books.

"Time, Temporality, Now: Experiencing Time and Concepts of Time in an Interdisciplinary Perspective" edited by Michael Flaherty (2013)

Flaherty, M. (Ed.). (2013). Time, Temporality, Now: Experiencing Time and Concepts of Time in an Interdisciplinary Perspective. Brill.

"The Future of Time: The Science, Art, and Spirituality of Time" by Peter Cochrane (2012)

Cochrane, P. (2012). The Future of Time: The Science, Art, and Spirituality of Time. Headline Publishing Group.

"A Brief History of Time" by Stephen Hawking (1988)

Hawking, S. (1988). A Brief History of Time: From the Big Bang to Black Holes. Bantam Books.

"The Order of Time" by Carlo Rovelli (2018).

Rovelli, C. (2018). The Order of Time. Riverhead Books.

"Time Reborn: From the Crisis in Physics to the Future of the Universe" by Lee Smolin (2013).

Smolin, L. (2013). Time Reborn: From the Crisis in Physics to the Future of the Universe. Houghton Mifflin Harcourt.

"Einstein's Dreams" by Alan Lightman (1992).

Lightman, A. (1992). Einstein's Dreams. Pantheon Books.

"The Fabric of the Cosmos: Space, Time, and the Texture of Reality" by Brian Greene (2004).

Greene, B. (2004). The Fabric of the Cosmos: Space, Time, and the Texture of Reality. Alfred A. Knopf.

"Now: The Physics of Time" by Richard A. Muller (2016)

Muller, R. A. (2016). Now: The Physics of Time. W. W. Norton & Company.

"The End of Time: The Next Revolution in Physics" by Julian Barbour (2000).

Barbour, J. (2000). The End of Time: The Next Revolution in Physics. Oxford University Press.

"Time: A Traveler's Guide" by Clifford A. Pickover (1998)

Pickover, C. A. (1998). Time: A Traveler's Guide. Oxford University Press.

"Time's Arrow and Archimedes' Point: New Directions for the Physics of Time" by Huw Price (1997).

Price, H. (1997). Time's Arrow and Archimedes' Point: New Directions for the Physics of Time. Oxford University Press.

"The Arrow of Time" edited by Lee Smolin (1993)

Smolin, L. (Ed.). (1993). The Arrow of Time. Springer.

"Time, Love, Memory: A Great Biologist and His Quest for the Origins of Behavior" by Jonathan Weiner (1999).

Weiner, J. (1999). Time, Love, Memory: A Great Biologist and His Quest for the Origins of Behavior. Vintage.

"The Map of Time: A Trip into the Marvelous History of the Wellsian Time Machine" by Félix J. Palma (2008)

Palma, F. J. (2008). The Map of Time: A Trip into the Marvelous History of the Wellsian Time Machine. Atria Books.

"The Discoverers: A History of Man's Search to Know His World and Himself" by Daniel J. Boorstin (1983)

Boorstin, D. J. (1983). The Discoverers: A History of Man's Search to Know His World and Himself. Vintage Books.

"Time Warped: Unlocking the Mysteries of Time Perception" by Claudia Hammond (2012).

Hammond, C. (2012). Time Warped: Unlocking the Mysteries of Time Perception. Canongate Books.

"Time: The Familiar Stranger" by J.T. Fraser (1987)

Fraser, J. T. (1987). Time: The Familiar Stranger. University of Massachusetts Press.

"Why Does E=mc2?: (And Why Should We Care?)" by Brian Cox and Jeff Forshaw (2009).

Cox, B., & Forshaw, J. (2009). Why Does E=mc2?: (And Why Should We Care?). Da Capo Press.

"Time Travel: A History" by James Gleick (2016)

Gleick, J. (2016). Time Travel: A History. Pantheon Books.

"The Time Paradox: The New Psychology of Time That Will Change Your Life" by Philip Zimbardo and John Boyd (2008).

Zimbardo, P., & Boyd, J. (2008). The Time Paradox: The New Psychology of Time That Will Change Your Life. Free Press.

"The Philosophy of Time" edited by Robin Le Poidevin and Murray MacBeath (1993).

This list encompasses a wide range of perspectives, including physics, philosophy, psychology, anthropology, and more, providing a comprehensive exploration of the subject of time and its nature.

Index: